NORTH ROSEDALE PARK

ONE HUNDRED YEARS OF HISTORY

Rose M. Love

North Rosedale Park
One Hundred Years of History
by Rose M. Love

Published and distributed by the North Rosedale Park Civic Association.
Address inquiries to the North Rosedale Park Civic Association,
18445 Scarsdale, Detroit, MI 48223. Website: nrpca.org

Cover and book design by Elena Farmer
Front cover, center photograph by David Edwards
Back cover photograph by Marsha Bruhn

ISBN: 978-0-578-80822-2

First edition, printed in the United States of America.

Printed by Ingram Content Group, 1 Ingram Blvd., LaVergne, TN 37086

CONTENTS

PREFACE

The life of a community is only as good as the people who are part of it. This book has evolved from a vast historical archive of letters, minutes, news articles, newsletters, court cases, albums, blueprints and photographs chronicling the life of North Rosedale Park and its representative organization, the North Rosedale Park Civic Association, since its founding. Tucked away in the Community House for years is a treasure trove of materials that, along with first-person narratives, has shaped this book.

What a privilege to be able to research these documents and come to appreciate the work of Park historians who preserved them for us. What a privilege to join in perpetuating the dream of a truly unique community and in leaving a legacy for those who follow us. To those of you who live in the Park and those to come, understand that it is your responsibility to maintain the Community House and its activities, to support the Civic Association in representing the interests of all of the residents, and to keep this neighborhood strong. The record speaks for itself.

Marsha Bruhn, The Legacy Project

FOREWORD

The Times Change but The Memories Endure

Happy Centennial North Rosedale Park!

One hundred years ago, when developer Henry Shelden planned a neighborhood in what was then 1920s Redford Township, he did so with the vision of a "garden suburb" that would feature architecturally detailed homes with a four-acre park and community house as the glue to hold the new neighborhood together. Despite the 100 years of good times and not so good times in our city, we've been fortunate to have a neighborhood that perseveres.

History shapes our future by connecting us to past lessons and, on behalf of the North Rosedale Park Civic Association Board of Directors, it's a privilege to serve our neighborhood during this defining centennial year. In the pages of this book, you'll find a chance to look back to move forward. North Rosedale Park was founded in 1919 in the aftermath of the 1918 flu pandemic with the first residents moving into newly built homes in 1920. It was a decade of change and Detroit was at the epicenter, a city growing faster than any other in the country. Those early residents laid the path for the talent and tenacity that we see today as we commemorate our anniversary and stay safe against the current global coronavirus pandemic. One hundred years later, we are fortunate to live in a diverse and active neighborhood that represents an array of voices and perspectives. It's not lost on me that 100 years ago this was far from the case, and as we reflect on the story of our community, we must do so authentically with equity and inclusion at the center and use our anniversary as a catalyst for lasting neighborhood transformation.

The NRPCA Board of Directors is deeply grateful for the leadership team of Rose Love, Tess Tchou, Marsha Bruhn, and the committed group of neighborhood volunteers that came together to form the North Rosedale Park Centennial Committee. Whether you still live in the neighborhood or have moved to another, we're connected to this corner of Detroit by a special park and Community House. I hope you read these pages and find opportunities to stay involved.

One hundred never looked so good, North Rosedale Park. Let's continue to be a neighborhood that bands together and ensure our legacy for the next generation.

With Gratitude,

Wendy Lewis Jackson
President
North Rosedale Park Civic Association

Introduction

In October 2019, I stumbled upon a document on the historic designation of Rosedale Park, our sister neighborhood across Grand River Avenue. If Rosedale Park was established in 1916, then how old was North Rosedale Park? I learned that 2019 was the 100th anniversary of the establishment of North Rosedale Park. That called for a celebration. A centennial committee was formed and plans were in the works for a yearlong celebration in 2020, including a book chronicling 100 years of history in the Park, a Rosedale Park Woman's Club reunion, a community picnic during June Day, a Home and Garden Tour, all culminating with the Party of the Century. By March 2020, the world was spinning upside down as the coronavirus spread across the globe. Plans for a grand celebration were canceled. Yet, the book project proceeded.

After a year of research – reading roughly 1000 *Rosedale Tattlers*, skimming board minutes and documents, nearly 40 interviews, hundreds of questions, consultations and poring over photos – the story of North Rosedale Park came into focus. While writing a book that covers 100 years is a tall order, it has been a thrill learning more about my neighborhood and those who call it home. Although I had never aspired to write a book (not every journalist wants to be an author), this project has whet my appetite.

As a person who enjoys history, I was engulfed in a big history lesson. Over this last year, I could sense the pride in the accomplishments of so many North Rosedale Park residents, many noted leaders in their respective fields. As I looked at the events that shaped the United States and Detroit, I saw how those events played out in North Rosedale Park, as leaders wrote letters, signed petitions, took legal action and formed alliances to protect and advocate for residents here and in northwest Detroit. While at the same time, I could feel the frustration and disappointment when problems continued to resurface over the decades.

North Rosedale Park traces its beginning to two companies, Clemons, Menard, Knight Co. and H.D. Shelden's Sons. The Sheldens envisioned a subdivision unique from other developments, a neighborhood with single-family homes on large lots and land set aside for a school, park and community center. Pioneer families from Detroit were enticed by the slogan, "Out of the Smoke Zone into the Ozone," to move to Redford Township for clean, fresh air and suburban living in the country.

Those pioneers organized and created an association and took advantage of the land set aside by the developers to build a clubhouse. It was replaced by the present Community House – the hub of activity for the various programs and events sponsored by the North Rosedale Park Civic Association, Rosedale Park Woman's Club and other auxiliary organizations, like the American Legion Post 390. The park surrounding the Community House saw plenty of activities as well. North Rosedale Park is unique as the only Detroit neighborhood with its own Community House and park, which many point to as the neighborhood's most important asset. It is the central location where residents from the neighborhood's east side (Ashton) can meet neighbors from the Park's west side (Evergreen) and all streets in between.

As I did research for the book, it became apparent that, if not for the Community House, it would have been difficult, and probably impossible, to have had access to such an accumulation of documents. Those documents, combined with the recollections and experiences of current and former residents, demonstrate that the commitment to building a better community is still evident among Park residents today.

All of these factors are why North Rosedale continues to be one of Detroit's premier neighborhoods. As our community eventually gathers to celebrate the Park's centennial, whether in 2021 or 2022, it will be a celebration of the past and the realization that this neighborhood thrives because residents continue to build on the foundation that began 100 years ago.

THE 1920S

Traveling northwest from downtown Detroit for nearly 12 miles or so through open countryside and farmland to the intersection of Mill Road and Grand River, one came to an area that resembled a hodgepodge of sorts. To the south was Rosedale Park, a relatively new subdivision, with a handful of stately brick homes scattered across the landscape. To the north was a vast sea of openness broken up by pavement here and there. The trees were bent slightly to the east from the winds that blew over the unoccupied fields. Absent was the smell of fumes clogging the air all too common in the city, while the smell wafting through the air was a strange mixture of grass, farm animals, flowers from a nearby greenhouse, and metal burning underneath the streetcars traveling down Grand River from Detroit to Redford and back again. About a half-mile west was a stream running parallel to the road, where local residents fished.

North Rosedale Park is that rare thing in an American city – a community where the folks next door are neighbors in fact as well as in name. This is the result of no happy accident. The first flower of a friendly community spirit does not come to full bloom without painstaking cultivation and care.

DON HAYDEN, North Rosedale Resident

In 1919, the area to the north was simply known as Rosedale Park No. 2, miles away from the big city and out in the country. Now, some 100 years later, North Rosedale Park is one of Detroit's premier neighborhoods, boasting of its own community house and surrounding park, beautiful stately homes and boulevards, and the neighborhood of choice for many of Detroit's movers and shakers, then and now.

Two Detroit mayors, several City Council members, judges, professional athletes, business executives, government leaders, entertainers, spiritual leaders and even a Michigan governor and Lt. Governor have all, at one time, called North Rosedale Park home.

That's **North** Rosedale Park!

How It All Began

The formation of North Rosedale Park is closely tied to the creation of Rosedale Park, its sister neighborhood across Grand River, which was developed in 1916. Then the entire area was known as Rosedale Park, no South Rosedale or North Rosedale in those days. Grand River, like many early roads in Michigan, followed the trail that Native Americans had used.

North Rosedale Park land purchase
Detroit Free Press, June 1919

Ad for Rosedale Park
"Out of the Smoke Zone into the Ozone"

Stretching from Detroit to Lansing, Grand River was known as the primary stagecoach and wagon freight route through central Michigan until the railroad was built.[1]

The earliest section of Rosedale Park was platted by the Rosedale Park Land Company in September 1916 on farmland in Redford Township, Michigan about 12 miles northwest of the center of Detroit. A portion of that land was purchased from Albert Stahelin, a farmer and florist who owned a nursery and greenhouse on Grand River. Stahelin, a street named in his honor, runs through both subdivisions.[2]

In the late 1910s, Redford Township was 36 square miles including a small portion of Southfield Township. The township stretched from Eight Mile Road (called Baseline) to Joy Road and from Greenfield Road to Inkster Road.

Clemons, Knight, Menard and Paul Company, the parent company of Rosedale Park Land Company, was responsible for a number of developments including Greenfield Park, Glendale Gardens, Glendale Courts, Beverly Hills, Rosedale Park and North Rosedale Park, concentrating its efforts near Grand River Avenue in what is now northwest Detroit. Rosedale Park and North Rosedale Park, developed as abutting neighborhoods on the south and north sides of Grand River, were by far the company's largest and most ambitious developments.[3]

The company's slogan, "Out of the Smoke Zone into the Ozone," was an enticement to city dwellers to leave their crowded, smoke-filled neighborhoods for clean, country living with access to streetcars, well-maintained local roads and healthy, clean air.

"The homeowners of Detroit are not responsible for the congested conditions of the city. To bring the right people to a suburb there must be something to attract them. The living conditions must be right. Rosedale Park makes this appeal and supplies a real want. It was created for the Home Lover. For the man and woman who would like to live in a good neighborhood but cannot, or will not, pay the city prices," read a Clemons, Knight, Menard Company ad in the May 1919 *Free Press*.

It wasn't hard to convince people to make a move. In the 1920s, Detroit was a bustle of activity as the home to 3000 major manufacturing plants, 37 automobile manufacturing plants and 250 automotive accessory manufacturing plants. As the 4th largest city in America with a population of 993,678, there were

Grand River looking west, 1916
Courtesy of Redford Township Historical Commission

Subdivision No. 2, Recorded September 20, 1919

lots of people, crowded housing and plenty of smog.

The area was bounded by the well-traveled Grand River (also called Lansing Road), with bumpy, narrow pavement on its south side and interurban train tracks on its north side, providing the only means of public transportation. The interurban system, operated by the Detroit United Railway, was an electric railway with streetcars that ran in Detroit and between the city and surrounding communities.

The sons of H.D. Shelden, a prominent Detroit businessman, were financiers turned real estate developers. The company purchased land north of Grand River and laid out Rosedale Park Subdivision No. 2 in 1919, followed by No. 3 in 1920 and Nos. 5-12 in 1924.

Early North Rosedale Park along Bretton Dr. with first four homes in view

The first four homes built in the Park

18380 Bretton

18420 Bretton

This New
Residence
For Sale
in

ROSEDALE PARK

The Dutch Colonial type of house makes such an appeal to
home lovers that we are positive this delightful home—pictured
above—will be eagerly sought for during the next few days.

Out
of the
Smoke Zone
into the
Ozone

Regarding the interior: On the first floor is found a center
hall, living room, sun room, dining room, breakfast room,
kitchen and butler's pantry. On the second floor are four bed-
rooms, two baths and large sleeping porch.

This home is on Stratford Drive, one of Rosedale Park's
handsome 100-foot boulevards.

CLEMONS, KNIGHT, MENARD CO.

725-727 Farwell Bldg.   Cadillac 7266

18442 Bretton

18480 Bretton

These later expansions created the present boundaries of North Rosedale Park – McNichols (Six Mile Road) to Grand River, and Southfield Road (then Mill Road) to Evergreen. The only exception was a rectangular area north of Puritan between Glastonbury (then Harrison Blvd.) and Sunderland. H.D. Shelden's Sons was unable to purchase that land at a fair price. It wasn't until the 1970s that this area, encompassing Greenview, Avon and Stahelin streets, was included in the North Rosedale Park footprint.

During that first year – the winter of 1919 – four homes were built near the east end of Stratford Drive (now Bretton Drive). Those first homes at 18380, 18420, 18442 and 18480 Bretton were model homes and weren't occupied until rented out a couple of years later. The first known residents were Fred and Edith Herbert, who moved into their home at 16900 Evergreen near Six Mile Road in November 1920. Herbert, a civil engineer, was the superintendent of the area and worked for the Sheldens and was responsible for the engineering projects to enhance the neighborhood and for planting.

"On the whole, the Shelden plan was radically different from that followed by Detroit realtors at that time. It is not to be supposed that altruism was a guiding motive but the distinct feeling of pride in the development, coupled with the belief that the venture would be most profitable if it also appealed to the pride of those who bought ... The Sheldens adopted a policy of selecting as pioneers residents those whom they believed would probably be most desirable." Harry St John, author of "The Beginning of Rosedale Park," October 1934 *Tattler*

Indeed, the Sheldens' plan included many features that contributed to North Rosedale Park being unique from so many other subdivisions. Property was landscaped. Large lots were set aside for a school and community park, that later played a significant role in the development of the community. Streets with boulevards were intentionally designed to break up the straightness of the lines to discourage through traffic.

House under construction (undated)

Homes were required to be two or three stories tall with no flat roofs. Minimum construction costs were required, ranging from $6500 to $8000 depending on the property's location within the subdivision. Sales were limited to members of the Caucasian race (more on this later). The developers also priced property to discourage speculators, and carefully selected pioneer residents they believed would be able to maintain their mortgage and be assets to the community.

"Rosedale Park was not a 'per chance' real estate development. It was, to say the least, a well thought out development," according to Charles Erickson, business manager of H.D. Shelden's Sons. "We wanted to put on the market something that would be a credit to the company, as well as a credit to those who invested in home building … We wanted a type of development that would attract not the factory workmen but those with a little more economic security, and those who can afford the time for suburban living.

"We also felt that in order to protect the homeowners, rigid building restrictions should be enforced. From the architectural and artistic layout of the park, we tried to break away from the more common type of just parallel lines. We knew the secret of success from the sales end of it … would be beauty and charm. We are proud of Rosedale and we feel that it is ideal in suburban home building." (From Georgina Lannin's school paper on the economic development of Rosedale Park)

While the developers provided many amenities – water supply, sewers, paving and streetlights – there were many things that residents lacked. For one, there was no provision for garbage disposal and other waste. Mail was delivered to mail boxes on Grand River. Police protection was nearly non-existent. Though the area was equipped with fire hydrants, the Detroit Fire Department was summoned by telephone and came only with the assurance of a $50 fee backed by a responsible guarantee. Transportation to and from the area was limited to interurban cars that ran infrequently and at irregular intervals. Other problems included flooding during heavy rains due to inadequate storm drain capacity and no snow removal, which sounds all too familiar.

Then there was the help. Keeping a maid was difficult as residents were responsible for transporting maids to and from their homes by automobiles. Schools were distant and overcrowded. Grocery and department stores were reluctant to make deliveries to a few families in an area that was miles away in the country.

So much for leaving the smoke zone and entering the ozone.

Based on the lack of conveniences, which were readily available in the city, these early residents were often called pioneers.

North Rosedale Park Pioneers

Mr. & Mrs. Harry Archbold (16518 Warwick) – Moved to the Park in 1925. Archbold dubbed "Mayor of Rosedale Park;" editor in the 1930s of *Rosedale Tattler*. First realtor in the Park with business on Grand River near Warwick; compiled and published the Rosedale Directory.

Karl and Gertrude Brede (15728 Rosemont) – Moved to the Park in 1921.

Cyril and Mary Browne (18823 Gainsborough) – Lobbied education leaders to construct Cooke School.

Harry and Maud Heiby (18697 Gainsborough)

Fred and Edith Herbert (16900 Evergreen) – Moved to the Park in 1920 and considered the first permanent residents. Herbert was the Shelden company's area superintendent.

Jacob and Mae Judson (16241 Westmoreland and 18741 Bretton) – Judson, lumberman and homebuilder, was first Civic Association president, 1923-25.

Lewis and Ethel Judson (19420 Gainsborough) – Built the 10th house in the Park.

Raymond and Edna LaBarre (Edinborough) – LaBarre was Association's first treasurer, 1924.

Jack and Sara Lillie (19271 Lancashire and 16590 Plainview) – Moved to the Park in 1925. Lillie was NRPCA president, 1931-33. Worked for Harry Archbold Realty.

Roscoe and Lona Merchant (15919 Avon) – Merchant was building chairman, overseeing construction of the Community House in 1939.

Edward and Grace Nyland (16565 Edinborough) – Moved to the Park in 1923.

John and Adella Patrick (16503 Huntington)

Arthur and Reta Siebert (18896 Gainsborough) – Siebert was NRPCA president, 1936-37. Lobbied education leaders to construct Cooke School.

Frank Day and Alice Smith (16222 Warwick) – Smith served as NRPCA attorney; instrumental in winning Association's legal battles including City maintenance of boulevard islands. Judge on Wayne County Circuit Court.

Grover and Janet Smith (Rosemont) – Moved to the Park in 1921.

Walter and Lillian Phipps (18380 Bretton)

C.G. Rowlette (18420 Bretton, one of the four original homes, and later, 16615 Shaftsbury)

Frank and Hazel Solar (19350 Gainsborough) – Solar was NRPCA's vice president in 1924, and Toolcraft editor of the *Free Press*.

Clarence and Louise Weaver (18696 Gainsborough and later 16196 Shaftsbury) – Weaver was instrumental in organizing NRPCA; president, 1925-27. First president of Grand River-Redford Federation of Community Associations.

Two other individuals, **Harry M. St. John (18825 Lancashire)** and **Alban Norris Sr. (15745 Rosemont)** played integral roles as *Rosedale Tattler* editors. St. John was also the Park historian.

Shortly after the platting of North Rosedale Park began, real estate activities came almost to a halt. From January 1920 to July 1921, the United States, United Kingdom and other countries experienced a post World War I recession, complicated by the re-entry of millions of veterans into the economy.

It would take several years before new construction would resume in North Rosedale Park. By the end of 1923, there were about 12-15 homes mostly on or near Gainsborough and some on Stratford (now Bretton).

Gainsborough, looking east from Warwick, Spring 1923

Though small in number, the neighbors banded together and really got to know each other, albeit by eavesdropping on the telephone line shared by 12 households. "Wall phones or hand phones, it made no difference – we were all on the same line – even the doctor. One would think there were a million when you wanted the line. Then too, it was just a bit tempting – and – we tried not to miss very much of these serious conversations. It no longer remained a secret – for when we met at the Thimble Club – the conversation would come out – too good to keep. We weren't at the stage yet – where we could say 'I won't talk.' " (From "Little Things We Used to Do" by Louise Weaver, March 1936 *Tattler*)

Moving forward, the Sheldens' plan was to build homes with a financing plan attractive to those hard hit by the recession. The subdivision greatly expanded in size as land was purchased and houses built in 1924. By the end of the decade, there were 400 families in the Park.

Horace Maynard, an early resident, was introduced to Rosedale Park in the early 1920s. "My first connection with what was then a far-out subdivision was made early in 1921. My wife persuaded me to take her to the Builder's Show. Before we escaped, we had been interested in North Rosedale for future residence. A salesman drove us out the next weekend

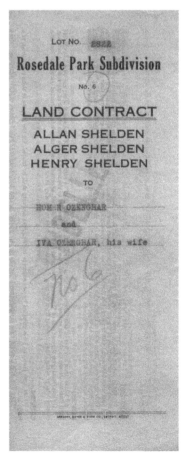

Cancelled land contract, 1932

and pointed to a distant corner lot, which he stated contained a large elm on the southwest corner of Avon and Puritan. There were no pavements laid as yet except Bretton Drive, and the slush and mud were too deep to permit a closer inspection. We soon signed up for the purchase on installments of 1% per month.

"Eventually Avon was paved and a sidewalk laid, and we found the tree was beyond the northeast corner outside the limits of North Rosedale. In December of 1924, ground was broken for the colonial residence presently standing there and in late May of 1925 we moved in with our two children – Bud and Mary – ages 5 and 2. The Ross Merchants, our only neighbors, invited us over to dinner the first night. Before the first summer was over, I began attending meetings of the association and remember helping to build a wooden sidewalk from the curb to the entrance of the old frame clubhouse." The Maynards lived at 15967 Avon.

Rosedale Park vs. Rosedale Park

Rosedale Park residents south of Grand River had already organized, creating the Rosedale Park Improvement Association (RPIA). As residents began moving into North Rosedale Park, RPIA invited its neighbors to the north to attend its meetings and join the organization. Although residents had many problems in common and thought they could work together, it was apparent they could not function as one since their interests were different, and, at times, in direct opposition.

The location of a school was a prime example. In laying out the subdivision, the Sheldens set aside a wooded area (parcel 2003) bounded by Avon Road, Harrison Blvd. (now Glastonbury), Grand River Avenue and Lancashire Road for a school. Since the location would require children from Rosedale Park to cross Grand River Avenue, Rosedale Park residents were opposed.

That location was quickly dismissed. Instead, a site on the south side of Grand River just east of Southfield Road (then called Mill Road) in the Grandmont area was selected, and Greenfield School (now Edison School) was built to meet the needs of Redford District No. 2.

The wishes of the majority, Grandmont and Rosedale Park, outweighed the concerns of the small group of residents living in North Rosedale Park, who were not happy. Complicating matters, children in North Rosedale Park also attended different schools because of school district boundaries. It would take several more years before North Rosedale would get its own school.

North Rosedale Park Organizations Take Shape

The year of 1923 saw the beginning of two organizations that have defined North Rosedale Park – the North Rosedale Park Civic Association and the Rosedale Park Woman's Club.

The Rosedale Park Woman's Club was incorporated in 1923 to organize social activities, and conduct literary and charitable works. Starting with 15 women at its first meeting at the home of Mary Browne, the organization grew to more than 500 by its 50th anniversary in 1973.

For more than half of its existence, the North Rosedale Park Civic Association (NRPCA) was an all-male organization. The Association operated independently yet cooperatively with the Woman's Club, which included many of the members' wives. Organized in the home of Frank Day Smith in 1923, NRPCA incorporated in September 1924. Under the new structure, the first officers were Jacob Judson as president; Frank Solar as vice president; Clarence Weaver as secretary; and Ray LaBarre as treasurer. Later that month, directors were chosen from the 26 households that paid the $10 membership dues.

The Association was formed to address a number of issues:

Woman's Club Community Picnic in the Park, July 4, 1924

- Building a local school
- Transportation to and from existing schools
- Building a clubhouse
- Obtaining ownership of the park in the name of the association
- Whether to seek annexation to Detroit or to incorporate as a village
- Increasing membership and development of a social program
- Securing door-to-door mail delivery
- Installing street signs and house numbers
- Obtaining more adequate police protection than provided by the sheriff's office

Woman's Club at 19440 Bretton, May 5, 1926

Minutes of North Rosedale Park Civic Ass'n held at the residence of Mr. J. G. Judson, Friday Evening, September 13th, 1924.

1.

Meeting opened at 8:40 P.M. by President J. G. Judson.

2.

Purpose of meeting to form a corporate association to function in place of voluntary association which has been conducting meetings since July 1923.

3.

President J. G. Judson and Mr. L. E. Barnett explained why the corporation is necessary and advisable.

4.

Mr. F. Day Smith read the statutes governing Non-Profit Corporate Associations, also read from sample form filled in according to what he thought should be the scope and action of the North Rosedale Park Civic Association.

5.
General Discussion.
Motion duly made and carried that we incorporate as the "North Rosedale Park Civic Association."

6.

Pres. J. G. Judson appointed Mr. F. D. Smith and Mr. L. E. Barnett to prepare and file necessary papers for corporation.

7.

Pres. Judson advised election of new officers in order.

8.

Motion was duly made and carried that same officers and committees that served in voluntary association during 1924 and to date be retained. They are:

Mr. J. G. Judson, President
Mr. C. L. Weaver, Secretary

School Committee

Mr. N. Arthur

Board votes to incorporate Civic Association, 1924

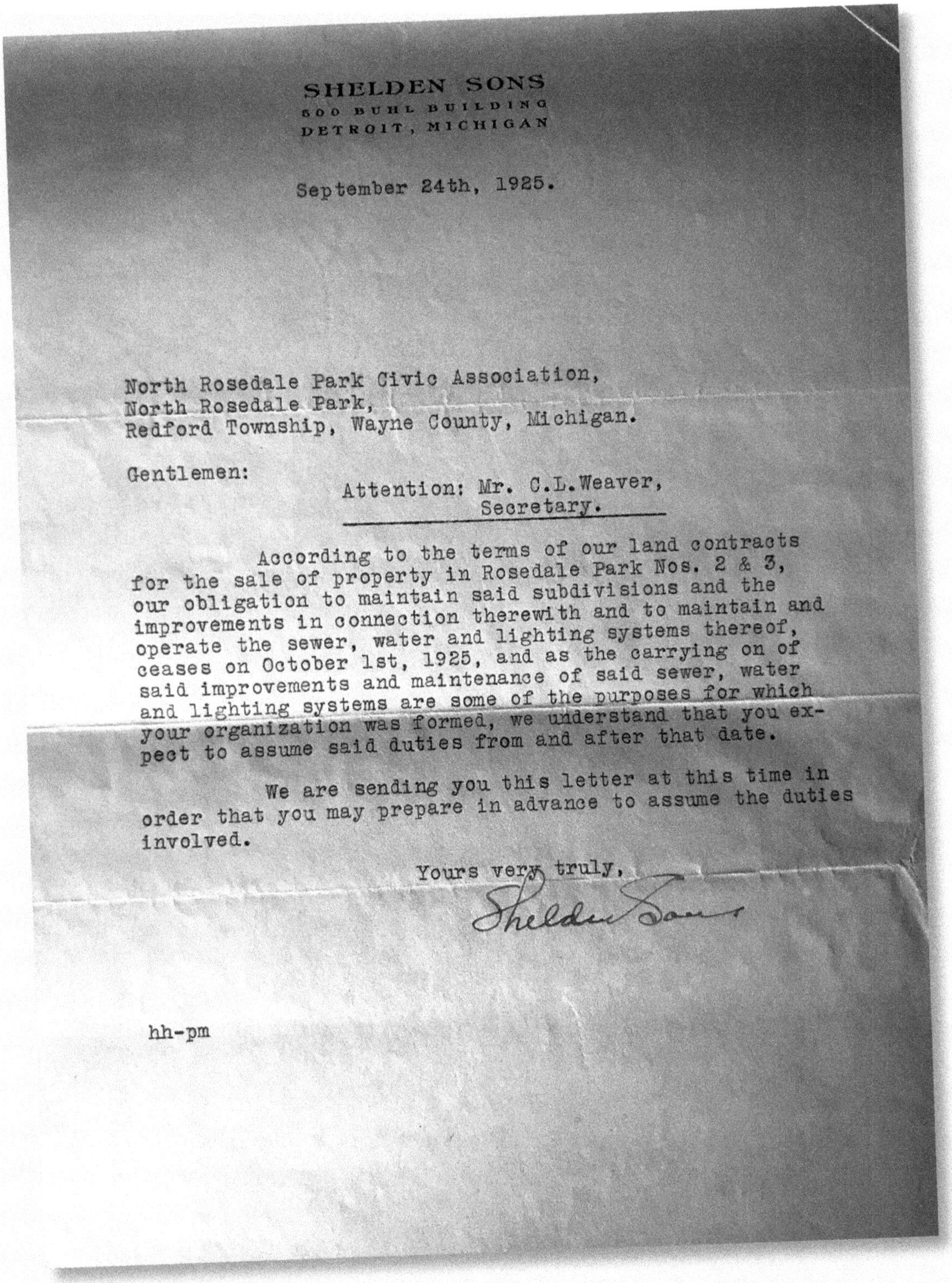

SHELDEN SONS
500 BUHL BUILDING
DETROIT, MICHIGAN

September 24th, 1925.

North Rosedale Park Civic Association,
North Rosedale Park,
Redford Township, Wayne County, Michigan.

Gentlemen:

Attention: Mr. C.L.Weaver,
Secretary.

According to the terms of our land contracts
for the sale of property in Rosedale Park Nos. 2 & 3,
our obligation to maintain said subdivisions and the
improvements in connection therewith and to maintain and
operate the sewer, water and lighting systems thereof,
ceases on October 1st, 1925, and as the carrying on of
said improvements and maintenance of said sewer, water
and lighting systems are some of the purposes for which
your organization was formed, we understand that you expect to assume said duties from and after that date.

We are sending you this letter at this time in
order that you may prepare in advance to assume the duties
involved.

Yours very truly,

Shelden Sons

hh-pm

Shelden Sons to turn over utilities maintenance to NRPCA, 1925

The school situation was the most pressing of those issues. The goal was to build a school in North Rosedale Park, so that children could attend a school close by and not be shuttled to several different schools. Cyril Browne and Art Siebert regularly attended the Redford School Board meetings and were successful in convincing the board to build a school in North Rosedale. However, that would require a portion of North Rosedale to be added to the Redford District No. 2 boundaries. It also required the support of Rosedale Park residents, who had only higher taxes to gain.

After weeks of cajoling and campaigning, enough signatures were obtained, and the petitions were filed in December 1924 and granted soon after. Plans for construction began immediately, but soon began to unravel.

In July 1925, it became apparent that the plans for the school might be in jeopardy. Taxpayers in other parts of the district were alarmed about the increasing debt of the Redford School District and started a movement to elect a new board that would halt construction of the new school. The North Rosedale Park community got to work again, campaigning to retain the current board and keep hopes of a school alive. On election day, North Rosedale residents transported their neighbors in support of the current school board all day to the polls at Redford High School. Their efforts paid off, and the existing board was retained.

---

*"Detroit has a slogan – a seat for every child –
but that bunch in the northwest demands
a school for every child."*

The site for the Cooke School on Puritan was selected, and construction began in earnest in 1925. For some, the school seemed a bit ambitious for the small community of only 125 families. With the vote to annex to Detroit, the City also inherited the debts for school construction, which led City Councilman John Hall to say: "Detroit has a slogan – a seat for every child – but that bunch in the northwest demands a school for every child."

Before Cooke's construction, children from the Park were educated in a portable, a conventional, two-room structure so crowded that students in second through fourth grades attended only half days. Kindergarten and first-grade classes were held in the North Rosedale clubhouse. Students in fifth through eighth grades were transported to the old Burt School, which eventually became a branch of Receiving Hospital.

When Cooke School became a part of the Detroit education system, major problems emerged. The contractor built the school on its natural elevation, below street level, which led to flooding, and the building had heating and sewage problems. Later, Detroit school officials learned that the school was built on private property. The Redford school district had failed to purchase the property. After those problems were resolved, the school was dedicated in March 1927.

Lyle Reading remembered the 1928 graduation party for Cooke School held in the clubhouse: "In order to get the boys to dance with the girls, Mrs. Morse would take one of the boys and dance him around the room. Afterwards she would tell him what a good dancer he had been and then immediately planted him in the arms of one of the girls. We thought we were some dancers. The following year, we attended weekly dancing lessons in the clubhouse. We learned the Waltz and the Two-Step. We danced to such tunes as Soft Light, Blue Heaven ..."

In addition to having a neighborhood school, transportation was another factor that led to the creation of the NRPCA. Transportation to the two public schools and the parochial school that Park residents attended, Grandmont, Burt and St. Mary's of Redford, was provided by the Sheldens for free. However, the Sheldens wanted

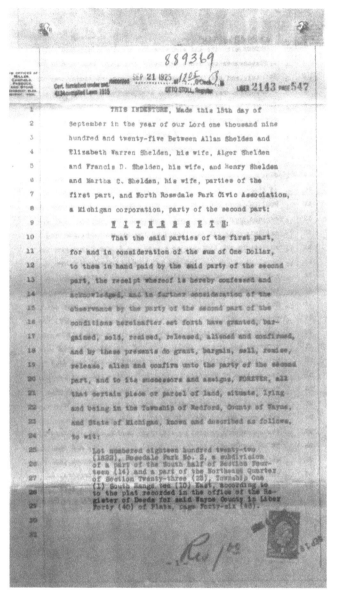

Transfer of park from the Sheldens to NRPCA
September 15, 1925

to turn over the bus to the residents along with $2000 for operations and maintenance for the 1924-25 school year.

While Rosedale Park residents wanted no part of the deal, North Rosedale Park assumed responsibility. However, the transportation situation quickly turned sour. Although $2000 seemed sufficient, by March the funds were nearly exhausted. The cost of insurance was high. The bus needed new tires, and the cooling system froze, causing the cylinder block to crack. To finish out the school year, the committee arranged for bus service with the Detroit Department of Street Railways (DSR). The banged-up bus was presented to an unsuspecting Redford School Board.

The Center of the Community

When the Shelden family mapped out the subdivision, plans included an area intended as a site for community use and a clubhouse, parcel 1822. The thickly wooded area covered a large city block. The site – bounded by Scarsdale (then Woodstock Road), Glastonbury (then Harrison Blvd.), Bretton (then Stratford Blvd. or Narragansett Drive) and Avon – was an ideal backdrop for community activities.

In the early days, the men gathered for a game of horseshoes, while the women sewed and made sure the men stayed out of trouble. Eventually, that led to Saturday afternoon picnics and evening campfires. "The men – supper time or dinner time – horseshoe was quite the thing and we would call and call – and dinner would grow cold – but play horseshoes they must," said Louise Weaver, who lived on Gainsborough.

Construction of the old clubhouse, 1924

Many of the early residents had the impression that the Sheldens would build a clubhouse on the site, thinking that they could then take in a weekly movie and enjoy a Sunday afternoon family skating party and potluck dinner. That was not to be. Therefore, in fall 1924, Frank Day Smith and Frank Solar led an effort to build a temporary structure until a more permanent building could be constructed.

According to Park historian Harry M. St. John, the building cost $2,000 with money raised through donations, fundraising, and a $200 loan, and was completed in less than three months. The construction involved nearly everyone living in the Park. With the exception of a few details, the work was performed by volunteers who were bankers, lawyers and salesmen by day, almost anything but carpenters.

"With everyone acting as construction engineer and boss, things moved rapidly," said Frank Solar, the Toolcraft Editor for the *Free Press* and a Park resident. "There were hammers all over the place. Every man and boy brought a couple of hammers, but squares, levels, and good sharp saws were hard to find.

"Everyone was ambitious. We worked early and late. Even the moon helped on this job, shining several evenings as bright as day. Messengers had arrived several times with information that if we did not get home to dinner we could stay and work all night. The old clubhouse, however, furnished a place for all to have a good time and become good friends and neighbors, and reports of good fellowship emanating from the old Clubhouse sold out the subdivision and made Rosedale Park the most talked of and most desirable place to live in the city of Detroit." (*Rosedale Tattler*, April 1940)

The clubhouse's opening was kicked off just before Christmas 1924 with a pair of keno parties, followed by the NRPCA meeting in January 1925, its first in the new building.

The first clubhouse was a single long room, 26 x 50 feet, heated by a coal stove at either end. Two years after the clubhouse was built, the remaining debt was paid. The Woman's Club was credited with helping raise the funds to retire the debt through a series of dinners and entertainment.

While the clubhouse became a hub of activity, so did the park surrounding the building. The first mention of the park being used for a skating rink was during the winter of 1927-28, and a playground for baseball in spring 1928. What quickly became a yearly tradition involved several Park residents hooking up water hoses and flooding a portion of the park to create two rinks. Once the water froze, residents flocked to the park for ice skating and hockey.

No group of Association leaders could claim success without an addition to the clubhouse during its term. At a cost of $1466.94, improvements to the clubhouse added a 20 x 16 foot annex with a new entrance to provide for dressing rooms, lavatories, furnace, kitchen, and a new ventilation system. The Woman's Club pledged $500 or one-third of the cost. Nearly ten years later in 1938, plans came together to build a larger, more permanent structure to accommodate the laundry list of activities.

Clubhouse with new addition

Like North Rosedale, Rosedale Park too had a wooded area donated by the developers. Early talk about building a clubhouse on the site never materialized. Eventually, the land, now Stoepel Park at West Outer Drive and Evergreen, became property of the City of Detroit.

In North Rosedale, the clubhouse and park owned by the Association have remained the center of activity, bringing together neighbors and creating a sense of community. Even today, the major selling point of North Rosedale is the Community House and its seven-acre park, unique among Detroit neighborhoods.

Village vs. Annexation

During the winter of 1924-25, there was talk of petitioning the City of Detroit to annex 40 square miles of land between Five Mile and Eight Mile roads. As residents gave further consideration to the idea, it was apparent that Rosedale Park residents would incur higher tax rates on top of already high property assessments.

That led to a group of North Rosedale residents floating the idea of incorporating Rosedale Park as a village to include Southfield to Evergreen and Six Mile to Schoolcraft. After careful study, it was determined that the village idea was not economically feasible. At a combined meeting of residents in the proposed area, it was apparent that there was not widespread interest in becoming a village, outside of North Rosedale Park. With that, the dream of Greater Rosedale Park died.

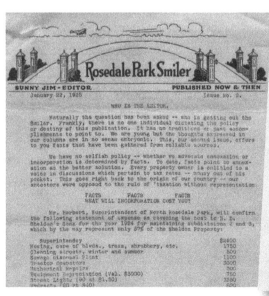

Rosedale Park Smiler, January 22, 1925

The Rosedale Growler, January 1, 1925

As the discussion for and against incorporation ensued, precursors to the *Rosedale Tattler* sprang up. *The Rosedale Growler* came first in support of the village proposal. Some months later, *The Rosedale Park Smiler*, though short-lived, was published in opposition to incorporation. Once the village idea was rejected, its publication ceased.

The *Growler* was not the official publication of the Association but was used on occasion as a vehicle to communicate to residents. In fact, the *Growler* became a welcome sight and a source of comic relief for residents whenever it appeared. The publication was edited by Josh Hague, under a pseudonym, and existed from 1924 to 1926. Considerable effort was spent trying to determine the editor's identity. Several residents were accused, including Frank Day Smith who quickly denied his involvement.

"We were made aware of the Community Association a few weeks later through the delivery of a flyer or photo entitled *The Rosedale Growler*. The only item, which has stuck in my memory was to the effect that attorney Frank Day Smith was to be presented a Cadillac limousine by the Association in gratitude for his outstanding legal services to the Restrictions Committee. My reflection at the moment was that this must be a fine mutual back-scratching outfit. I wonder what dues they demanded and who was to get the next present. Meeting Frank Day – later to be Judge Smith – soon thereafter, I learned more about him and that he cooked up these items and published *The Growler* himself." Horace Maynard, *Rosedale Tattler* January 1964

Annexation to Detroit seemed inevitable. However, that posed some significant problems for North Rosedale Park residents. In September 1925, the Sheldens notified the Association of their intention to cease public services on October 1 and turn over all equipment to residents to dispose of as they saw fit. Up to this time, the Sheldens had supplied water, and taken care of sewage disposal and streetlights by purchasing electricity from the Detroit Edison Company.

Rosedale Tattler, November 1929 issue

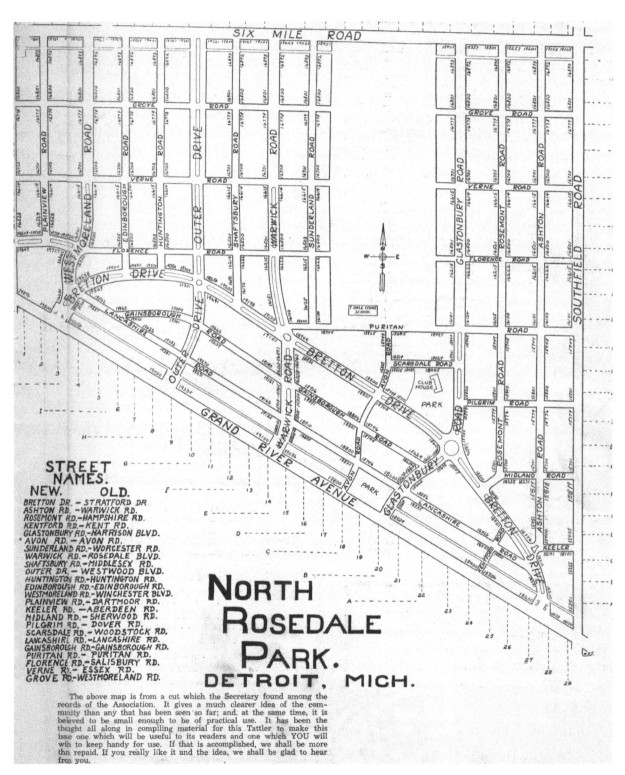

North Rosedale Park map with former and current street names

Association officials knew that the City of Detroit would not provide municipal services until sometime in 1926. The Association then negotiated with the Redford Township Board to provide all essential services until they could be taken over by the City of Detroit. A year earlier, the Sheldens had turned over the water system to the Detroit Board of Water Commissioners that provided city water at premium rates.

Following conversion of the City's water system, the Board of Water Commissioners informed Park residents that a water meter must be installed in homes and that galvanized iron pipes must be replaced with lead pipes. For months, residents resisted the Water Board and questioned if it would withhold water from residents who refused. Now, some 95 years later, the City of Detroit has embarked on a multi-year effort to gradually replace lead service lines and encourage residents to remove lead pipes in their homes and replace them with copper pipes.

In October 1925, the 35,000 residents in Rosedale Park, Five Points and Brightmoor voted overwhelmingly in favor of annexation. Rosedale Park had joined the big city.

The annexation vote had a devastating effect on Redford Township, reducing its area from 36 to 11.2 square miles. In addition, 17 of the 21 district schools, including Redford High School, came under the Detroit Board of Education, bringing 5000 students into the district. Redford was left with fewer than 450 students. Voters in Redford agreed to pay tuition for students to attend Detroit schools until a new Redford Union High School was built.[4]

Detroit had its eye on additional land but was blocked as Redford Township was given charter status by the Michigan legislature. As Detroit continued to gobble up other communities, Hamtramck and Highland Park resisted Detroit's overtures and remained self-governed, even though they were tucked in the middle of Detroit.

North Rosedale Again Leads the Way

The following month, newly elected NRPCA president C.L. Weaver led the way in developing a coalition of community associations to represent area residents and work with the City of Detroit on expanding municipal services into the area. The Grand River-Redford Federation of Community Associations, organized in November 1925, was an executive committee of delegates from North Rosedale, Rosedale Park (then called South Rosedale Park), Redford, Strathmoor, Grandmont and Homewood. Other associations joined later. Weaver was elected president.

On January 15, 1926, the federation invited Detroit officials to a banquet in Redford the day before the annexation became official. Detroit Mayor John Smith and most of his department heads attended and pledged their full cooperation. The first indication of that partnership was the announcement that City street cars would travel out Grand River as far as Redford beginning at 6 a.m. the very next day.

Although the federation existed for only about six years, it is believed that it saved residents several million dollars and handled concerns like schools, streets, lighting, water and sewer, and fire and police protection promptly and efficiently. The federation was successful in lobbying for the construction of the Southfield sewer, revision of telephone rates, and defeat of a bill by City Council member John Nagel to allow the Council to assess residents the cost of improvements in the newly annexed area. Again, the NRPCA led the way in lobbying against the measure.

Nagel's proposal was defeated twice, but he was not deterred. Sometime later, Nagel needed support from the Redford area to keep the proposed Rouge Park on the city's west side. After some negotiations, the Grand River-Redford Federation agreed to support the Rouge Park plan only after Nagel agreed to drop his assessment proposal. The deal worked.

After the annexation became official, one of the first steps was to change the names of streets to avoid duplication of street names in other parts of the city. Residents gave their input and a committee led by Harry M. St. John negotiated with the City Engineer's Office to finalize the renaming.

Another complication created by the annexation was what would happen to the wooded lot or the parkland. The Association approached the Sheldens to retain the lot as property of North Rosedale Park prior to the vote. Action was brought against Redford Township, bringing to light that the township had taken no action to maintain or enhance the park. The township had no interest in the matter and set aside the dedication by judicial decree on September 18, 1925. The land was then deeded by the Sheldens to the NRPCA with the stipulation that it would be used for park purposes.

The Way Forward

By 1926 the Association had 140 members representing about 90 percent of the residents in the area. As was the case then, the business of the Association was carried out by a small number of individuals. The Association instituted a social get-together occurring after each monthly business meeting as a means of increasing attendance, but some attendees timed their entrance to coincide with the end of business meetings.

In May 1926, the board authorized the creation of a monthly newspaper and named Harry M. St. John its first editor. The first *Rosedale Tattler* was published in June 1926. The early *Tattlers*, written mostly by St. John, were simple – printed on one side on a single sheet of paper, no illustrations or advertising.

The next year, the first map and directory of North Rosedale Park was printed on cardboard, the creation of Walter Gates, who did door-to-door canvassing. As a result, Gates was able to bring more than 50 new members into the Association. By this time, there were 300 homes in the Park with 213 Association members and roughly 50 attending meetings.

In early 1928, the Association began to address telephone rates. Subscribers connected to the REdford telephone exchange, but who lived in Detroit, paid a 10-cent toll charge for every call to another Detroit exchange. An appeal went to the State Public Utilities Commission through the Grand River-Redford Federation, with North Rosedale Park leaders carrying the lion's share of the load. The Commission ruled in the Federation's favor in April 1928.

Association activities continued unabated through the end of the decade. In May 1929, the Junior Activities Committee was established and worked with the Woman's Club to organize youth and teen activities, which included dances, scouting activities and an annual Field Day.

That summer, residents petitioned the City of Detroit to modify the route of Outer Drive (previously named Westwood) so that it didn't run through Rosedale Park, but soon found out that the City had transferred its interest in that portion of Outer Drive to the Wayne County Road Commission. Efforts to change the Commission's decision were futile. Although the project was delayed for several years, eventually Outer Drive opened to traffic through Rosedale. This was one of the few battles North Rosedale Park leaders lost.

However, NRPCA leaders were not to be outdone when it came to plans to widen and pave Puritan Avenue from Southfield to Warwick. Plans called for Puritan to continue to Grand River by way of Bretton Drive, which required tearing out the parkway on Bretton. Once again, petitions were prepared and signatures gathered. After hearings by the City Council, it voted to indefinitely postpone further work on Puritan.

In 1929, the *Rosedale Tattler* also went through a makeover. From a single sheet of irregular size paper, the publication grew to eight pages with advertising as a regular feature. That same year, the Rosedale Directory with phone numbers of neighborhood households was created, an improvement on the first cardboard directory created in 1927. The editor of the improved *Tattler* and directory was Alban J. Norris.

THE 1930S

Detroit grew meteorically in the 1920s, fueled by entrepreneurial drive, innovation, and investment. Yet by the early 1930s, Detroit, like much of the country and parts of the world, was in the throes of the Great Depression. The stock market crash on October 29, 1929 created an economic tsunami as companies struggled to stay afloat, businesses were destroyed, and banks failed. Detroit's economy built on manufacturing was jolted. Detroit's automobile companies produced more than 5.3 million vehicles in 1929, only to see that number drop to 1.3 million by 1931. Detroit's population was roughly 1.58 million, while the number of unemployed stood at 223,568, the hardest hit of 19 major cities according to the U.S. Census Bureau.[1]

Homeless encampments, food lines, free medical clinics and clothing drives became the common sightings of the day. Many Detroiters were starving and barely sustained by relief benefits.[2] In the Park, family incomes shrank as individuals lost their jobs or saw their wages reduced. Bank accounts and personal fortunes were wiped out, foreclosures ensued, and residents left the Park unable to afford their homes.

Grand River and Seven Mile Road, 1926
Courtesy of Redford Township Historical
Commission

While many Park residents struggled, some were still compelled to help those in need and played an integral role in registering the unemployed in 1930. Those efforts were recognized by Detroit Mayor Frank Murphy, and many other cities soon followed Detroit's example.

With life upended for many, not everything came to a screeching halt. The Association successfully lobbied the City to install a modern street lighting system to replace the primitive system installed by the Sheldens, the subdivision developers. Streetlights were installed on Grand River from Joy Road to Berg Road in 1930, followed by

300 new streetlights in North Rosedale Park and another 300 in Rosedale Park the next year. Wiring was underground, with ornamental light poles replacing the poles that many considered unsightly.

Building on improvements made in the late 1920s, the Detroit Department of Street Railways (DSR) increased service on the Grand River line to accommodate the rise in passengers in the Redford area and extended the line to Seven Mile Road.

Ed Panzner, owner of Ed's Sweet Shop on Grand River and Warwick, later recalled, "In those days, streetcars served the way out citizenry and late in the evening it was common to see a coal car coupled to a streetcar to be delivered at the Stahelin's Nursery or the Redford Lumber Company. There were very few homes and the wooded areas were quite prominent then as were the wide-open spaces."

Association Activities
Continue Despite the Times

Plans were drawn to build an addition to the North Rosedale Park clubhouse that would increase the floor space by 50 percent. The inability to obtain a building permit delayed construction until fall 1930, but the new addition was finally dedicated in February 1931, a noble feat since it was completed during the early days of the Depression.

The clubhouse was command central for the myriad of NRPCA activities and meetings,

Woman's Club Officers, 1930-31
Back Row from l-r: Mrs. Deslierres, Mrs. Hornung, Mrs. Lillie; Middle Row: Mrs. Herbert, Mrs. Solar, Mrs. Ladendorf; Front Row: Mrs. Eddy, Mrs. Johnson, Mrs. Fairgrieve, Mrs. Putnam, and Mrs. Hudson

Woman's Club Annual Luncheon, May 27, 1931
Cast of "Her Brilliant Idea" performed by members (l-r): Mrs. Rennell, Mrs. Judson, Mrs. Perkins, Mrs. Vollbrecht, Mrs. Blowers, Mrs. Chase, and Mrs. Cunningham

Poster from first June Day 1930

June Day 1931, First prize went to the Hudson float by Association President Bill Hudson with his three children dressed in full naval outfits

including Boy and Girl Scouts, dance classes, open houses, bridge, and youth parties. Its sister organization, the Rosedale Park Woman's Club was equally as active with charitable works; monthly programs with speakers and musical performances, book reviews and legislation of interest to women; and support for Association efforts.

The one major event that managed to survive the Great Depression and several wars was June Day. On June 14, 1930, the Association held its first Rosedale Park Community Day, as it was called then, mostly focusing on children's activities. The day began with a parade, complete with a notable Detroit dignitary serving as the grand marshal, elaborately decorated floats, marching bands, clowns and participants in costumes. The parade was followed by competitions for children and teens ranging from races and relays to tug of war. Over the years, the event evolved and the name changed, but still included a parade, and children and teen activities. The more recent June Day events have included races and walks, a movie night for the youth and a concert for adults.

In October 1931, the Duplicate Contract Bridge Club was organized under the sponsorship of the Association. A year later, the Rosedale Park Junior League for young women over 18 was formed.

Another new group was formed in June 1933 – the Past Presidents' Club. Its first chair was C.L. Weaver with Harry St. John as vice chairman. Jack Lillie, the Association President, surmised that it was a good excuse for the past presidents and their wives to socialize and talk about the way it was and the way it should be.

A highlight that year was the first Rosedale Park Fair, a two-day celebration in September that attracted thousands of visitors. The activities included musical performances, dancing, kite and airplane flying, sewing exhibitions, crafts, flower and vegetable displays, pony rides, games and, of course, food.

Probably front and center in terms of activities was the all-male bowling league, formed in 1925 and expanded over the years. By 1938, the league included 26 teams with 130 bowlers. Bowling scores and standings were regular fixtures in the *Tattler* newspaper, at times taking up whole pages. The North Rosedale Park Orchestra was the highlight of the league's banquet in January 1939. The 11-member orchestra, formed just two months earlier, was led by conductor John Roney.

At the start of the NRPCA, individuals who wanted to bowl or take part in other activities had to be members of the Association. In 1930, the Association adopted a policy prohibiting the use of the clubhouse for political meetings promoting a candidate, with the exception of a member of the Association running for public office.

Residents Feel the Effects of the Depression

It wasn't until 1932 and 1933 that the economic climate began to seriously impact North Rosedale Park residents. As finances were squeezed, property owners focused on taxes, a common theme in 1930s *Tattlers*. Residents lamented that the City needed to reduce assessments based on decreasing home valuations. NRPCA directors were instructed to research the matter and return with their findings. A year later, the team presented a detailed tabulation of the original costs, replacement costs and the assessment of every residence in the Park. In May 1933, as a result of the committee's work, Association leaders believed that assessments on North Rosedale real estate and buildings should go down about 20 percent.

In addition to their taxes, Association members were desperately looking for other ways to save money and asked the NRPCA to lower the annual dues from $10 to $5. The proposal was rejected. As an alternative, the board recommended a 25-percent reduction if dues were paid promptly. That too was defeated by the membership by one vote in November 1932. The defeat didn't go over well, and the NRPCA saw its membership drop nearly 50 percent to 152 by April 1933. Eventually, the NRPCA membership relented and approved the 25-percent reduction, offering residents a $2.50 discount to anyone who paid their dues by January 15, 1934.

Although the area was still feeling the effects of the Depression, there were some good

W. Outer Drive between Florence and Verne, 1930s

signs. In 1933, 17 homes were built in the Park, and 55 lots were sold or changed hands in five weeks, more than had occurred in the previous four years. Many of the homes were built with financial assistance from local business organizations, in light of the failure of several Detroit banks.

By April 1935, North Rosedale experienced a building boom – the largest since 1924 – with 10 houses under construction and 30 more expected to begin in the spring. The building activity was described as the most healthy development since the collapse of the banks. Floyd McGriff, whose company published the *Tattler*, said no other part of Detroit was showing the same building activity as North Rosedale Park. The building boom continued in 1936, with 39 homes under construction and an estimated $2 million in investment.

As was the case over the years, many North Rosedale families moved to other homes in the Park. In September 1936, *Tattler* editor Harry Archbold recounted the names of more than 40 families that had moved from one house in the Park to another, some to newly constructed homes.

Georgiana Lannin wrote in a school paper on the economic development of Rosedale Park: "Rosedale is dominated by the professional and managerial classes whose utmost thought as suburbanites is to maintain the highest degree of civic pride and good fellowship for a worthy cause. The aftermath of four years of depression and the loss of a few small fortunes have not discouraged. He (North Rosedale) is still civic conscious and maintains his superiority as a leader in community fellowship."

North Rosedale Households

1930 · **525 homes**

1934 · **600 homes**

1936 · **800 homes**

1937 · **850 homes**

Not in Our Neighborhood

The NRPCA prided itself on maintaining community and building standards through the work of its Restrictions Committee. If committee members or Park residents saw signs of construction – like a bulldozer clearing land – they would spring into action and call for a meeting with the builder to ensure compliance with code and building restrictions. If builders resisted, the NRPCA didn't hesitate to pursue legal action as it did in June 1930, winning an injunction against a development company. The vigilance of that committee also averted the erection of a business on Bretton Drive. In 1931 alone, the committee closely tracked 78 homes to ensure that contractors followed the law.

While most of the committee's work focused on residential and commercial construction, it was quick to address any actions that could diminish the character and beauty of the Park. When a group of real estate operators constructed large signs advertising their businesses in January 1938, legal action was pursued. A Circuit Court judge ordered the signs removed and restrained the parties from erecting billboards or advertising in the future that violated building restrictions.

In a role reversal, the NRPCA took the Sheldens – subdivision developers and establishers of the original building restrictions – to court to have their company demolish a long-vacated building on Glastonbury near Grand River. A visiting judge from Port Huron gave the Sheldens 45 days to destroy or remove the unsightly disgrace, which was used as the company's local headquarters and storage space.

NRPCA Mouthpiece

Whether the Association was focused on lawsuits, taxes, pressing national or local issues, or the comings and goings of residents, it could be found in the *Rosedale Tattler*, the Association's monthly newspaper. Like the *Detroit News*, the slogan could have been "Read the *Tattler*, You'll Know."

The *Tattler* communicated important matters – new City initiatives and actions, and NRPCA events and community projects – as well as rather mundane subjects: who was on vacation or had dinner or tea with whom; who was sick, engaged, getting married, just had a baby or had moved from or to the Park. *Tattler* editors were not shy about their feelings, often weighing in on local and political matters and the actions of the municipal government. Being politically correct was not the sentiment of the day. Sometimes the coverage was as stark as this headline in April 1934, 'Reg' Barnard Drops Dead, or the December 1935 report of the suicide of former resident Chester Bland.

The *Tattler* was also the vehicle for public rebukes of those who got out of line, especially children and teens and their parents. Numerous *Tattler* articles and editorials focused on speeding in the neighborhood, home and car break-ins, damage caused in buildings under construction, broken streetlight bulbs, riding bikes recklessly in the street, and vandalism to the clubhouse.

The NRPCA's Parks and Boulevard Committee noted in an April 1935 report that the poor condition of a number of trees in the Park was "aggravated by the building of deliberate fires in the hollow of the trees by youngsters of the subdivision." Residents of Bretton Drive near Kentford and those on Warwick between Bretton and Florence complained repeatedly of boys playing ball and making too much "noise, shouting and turmoil." City Parks Department signage was stolen and its inspectors ignored.

Even adults did not escape being called out. On a regular basis, *Tattler* editors, contributors and the NRPCA officers implored residents to pay their membership dues or rebuked members for not being active in Association activities, while extolling the many advantages of living in the Park.

Attorney Frank Day Smith's May 1934 letter to board president Arthur Nicklet emphasized another problem – the need for rules and regulations to control the late-night parties at the clubhouse. "It is common knowledge ... that extensive gambling is indulged in in the club house on meeting nights until early in the morning, where often large stakes are won and lost."

A Public Disgrace!, a flyer regarding vandalism, October 31, 1929

To manage excessive drinking, he recommended "supplying only enough beer to serve one bottle at each plate and no more."

In April 1932, the *Tattler* got its first advice columnist, Nellie Dale. A young man, 24, wanted to know if he and his girlfriend, who were both out of work, should get married. Her response: "Your financial condition certainly does not warrant you asking any girl to marry you now, and I'm quite sure that even should the young lady find work you won't care to have her support, if you have any pride at all."

The *Rosedale Tattler* (or maybe its editor) rose to national prominence when it received a letter from President-Elect Franklin D. Roosevelt seemingly in support of a much-discussed *Tattler* editorial by Harry Archbold in June 1932. Archbold had suggested that unemployment relief could be achieved by using unemployed individuals to address flood control and reforestation in the Mississippi Valley.

By the late 1930s, the *Tattler* took on a different feel. There were fewer articles on political and national concerns and greater focus on local concerns, like bus schedules and garbage collection, or the entire court findings in instances where the NRPCA had taken legal action.

A Woman's Club membership card, 1939

For the first time, there were photos of the newly elected officers of the Rosedale Park Woman's Club, and listings of committees and committee members. The March 1939 issue included the photo and story on Alice Smith (better known as Mrs. Frank Day Smith) becoming the first vice president of the Republican Women's Federation of Michigan. It is believed that this was the first time a woman's picture had appeared on the front page of the newspaper.

Another first happened in the September 1939 issue. As was the custom of the day, women were referred to by their husband's name, as in Mrs. Ross Merchant. This issue broke with that tradition and listed Lona W. Merchant as the president of the Rosedale Park Woman's Club. The change was short-lived.

Over the years, the number of members went up and down, mainly hovering in the 300s, except in 1932 and 1933 during the Great Depression.

Membership Totals

January 1931 • **302 members**

September 1932 • **248 members**

April 1933 • **152 members**

March 1937 • **330 members**

January 1938 • **314 members**

February 1939 • **393 members**

Top-Notch Education

During the spring of 1931, Rosedale residents were not satisfied with the education level of their children leaving the eighth grade at Cooke School and entering high school. The Association formed a special school committee and worked with local school officials for several years to raise the instructional standards. The result: adoption of a revised curriculum for Cooke School that was better suited to students' abilities.

Cooke School expanded with the west side addition along Stahelin Street from the conservatory in the front to the gymnasium in 1936. The cost of the addition was $118,000.

Redford High School on Grand River at McNichols was erected in 1920, with second and third additions built by the Redford Union School Board in 1924 and 1925. In 1931, the school was slated to get a $942,000 addition. There were months and months of delays, resurveys, appraisals, more legal wrangling, and back-and-forth negotiations with homeowners. Construction

Boy Scouts in front of Cooke School, 1929

was expected to take a year and accommodate 2400 pupils. It would include a new gym with a pool, library, and new cafeteria. (February 1931 *Tattler*)

A new addition to accommodate another 1200 students was slated for completion by September 1938 at a cost of $666,000. It was to include biology, chemistry and physics laboratories with lecture rooms, an art room, 14 classrooms, three study halls, two shops and a complete lunchroom department.

Bushnell Church Starts in the Park

In 1924, the Detroit Council of Churches sought to establish a Congregational church in the fast-growing northwest area. Although still rural, the area was changing with the development of surrounding subdivisions.

A small congregation, led by Rev. Irving Stuart, met in the home of Park residents Lillian and Walter Phipps for the first time on December 11, 1924. The congregation of about 40 people soon moved services to a nearby school. A constitution and by-laws were created the next year for the new congregation, which was named Bushnell Congregational Church. Rev. Eddy Treat became the first pastor in May 1926.

After years of fundraising and planning, ground was broken on January 1, 1939 for a church building on Southfield Road, south of Grand River. The first services were held in September 1939. Bushnell was the church home of many residents from the North and South Rosedale Park and Grandmont subdivisions.

North Rosedale Park: Where Leaders Are Made

Since its inception in 1923, the NRPCA had earned the reputation as a group of leaders and strong advocates for its residents and those in surrounding communities, in terms of securing municipal services or confronting a company skirting the building and construction restrictions. Once again, the NRPCA led the fight in opposition to the City of Detroit's proposed plan to discontinue operation of the Redford branch of Receiving Hospital and prevailed.

In 1936 and 1937, the Association opposed the City of Detroit on two fronts. First, the City suspended maintenance of the boulevards on four streets in the Park in 1936. For 10 years, City crews had cut the grass and shrubs, repaired the pavement and cleared out catch basins on Warwick, Bretton, Glastonbury and Westmoreland. It was the City's position that these were just ordinary streets, which would make property owners responsible for special assessments for street improvements.

After following the usual recourse of petitioning City leaders to no avail, the NRPCA, led by attorney Frank Day Smith, filed four lawsuits to compel the City to maintain the boulevards. Finally, in October 1938, the Wayne County Circuit Court ruled in favor of the NRPCA, requiring the City to recognize the streets as boulevards and maintain them as such. The ruling: The City, at its own expense, will maintain the four boulevard streets, repave and provide all necessary upkeep without cost to the residents. The NRPCA had claimed a long-fought victory.

Whereas the battle over boulevard maintenance raged on for nearly two years, the assessment issue was settled very quickly. In April 1937, the City assessed the NRPCA $49,990 for the clubhouse and parkland – an action promptly appealed by

Ask Recognition of 4 Boulevards

A large delegation representing the North Rosedale Park Civic Association Wednesday requested the Council to place itself on record to the effect that four streets in Rosedale Park are boulevards in law and fact.

The four streets are Warwick road, Bretton drive, Westmoreland drive and Glastonbury road.

If the Council formally declares these streets are boulevards, the City must pay for re-paving, care for the shrubs and trees in the parkways, and keep the parkway and lawns mowed, all at the City's expense. If they are only streets, the cost of this work must be paid by property owners.

Frank Day Smith, attorney and spokesman for the association, asserted these four streets possess all the attributes of boulevards. They are 100 feet wide, possess boulevard parkways and were platted as boulevards. Since this section was annexed to the city, in 1926, the City apparently treated them as boulevards by planting flowers and shrubs in the parkways and caring for them in other ways until this summer, when the Department of Parks and Boulevards refused to mow the parkway lawns.

The Council apparently was impressed with Smith's recital but hesitated to grant the petition as it might establish a costly precedent.

An estimate of the cost of re-paving the four streets as well as other alleged boulevards in South Rosedale Park is to be submitted to the Council Tuesday by the DPW. The Council is to make its decision on the petition at that time.

Newspaper article on boulevards dispute

the Association. The Board of Review unanimously approved the request on April 29, within the same month, exempting the land and clubhouse from taxes. However, the assessment issue wasn't resolved for good. It would come back again.

For many years, Rosedale Park residents picked up their mail from boxes located on Mill Road (now Southfield Road) near Grand River. In order to install mailboxes at the curb, the Association needed to have homes numbered in accordance with the Detroit system. Although difficult, the numbering was completed, but securing door-to-door mail delivery would come later.

Out With The Old, In With The New

By the late 1930s, the clubhouse was no longer sufficient to accommodate the myriad of activities and meetings sponsored by the Association and the Woman's Club – over 200 in any given year that included bridge tournaments, Wolf Cubs, Girl Scouts, dancing classes, bowling club, and private dances and parties.

In July 1938, a building committee was formed, headed by Ross C. Merchant. Blueprints were drawn, and a plan to finance construction with loans of at least $100 from members was announced. Subscribers received Participation Certificates issued by the Association in denominations of $25, with a redemption period of 10 years. About $30,000 was raised by the loans, although actual construction costs were closer to $40,000. To partially fill the funding gap, the Association suc-cessfully convinced the Sheldens to deed property bounded by Grand River, Glastonbury, Lancashire and Avon. The property had already been platted and sewers installed. The NRPCA planned to sell the lots, with proceeds going to construct a new Com-munity House.

In 1939, the NRPCA launched a second cam-paign to sell certificates to more recent Park residents

On March 29, 1939 ground was broken for the new community House in North Rosedale Park. Ross Merchant, chairman of the Building Committee, operated the steam shovel. Frank W. Speicher, a member of the Civic Association, supervised construction. On August 11, 1939, less than five months later, the association held its first meeting in the new building.

New Community House

to pay off outstanding construction debts. The funds would cover things like landscaping, driveway, concrete walk and concrete terraces. The fundraising goal was $3000, with certificates selling for $25, $50 or more, but rising costs put the amount needed at $4000.

Ground was broken for the new 90 foot x 62 foot Community House, designed by architect and Association member Morris Webster, on March 29, 1939. Residents looked forward to good times in the new building with its spacious assembly and dance room, stage, ladies' powder room, up-to-date kitchen, scout room and efficient boiler plant. This was a place for children to get acquainted with each other and one that could house two or three events at the same time.

In July 1939, the NRPCA met for the last time in the old clubhouse, which had served Park residents for 14 years and was sold for $375 and dismantled. On August 11, with the Community House nearing completion, the first meeting of the neighborhood association was held in the balcony, the only place in the building with electricity at that point. A grand opening was held on September 8 with Detroit City Council President Edward Jeffries Jr. as the speaker, followed by a community open house two weeks later.

In the October 1939 *Tattler*, general contractor Frank Speicher recognized the subcontractors and those involved with the Community House construction. That list included all Detroit-based companies and several North Rosedale Park residents. Once again, the men of North Rosedale had pitched in by obtaining building materials at cost.

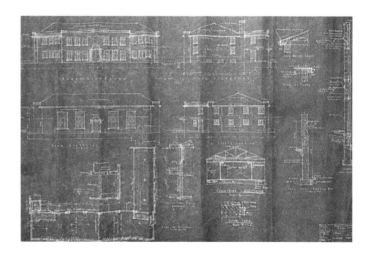

Blueprint of the Community House, 1939

THE 1940S

As the U.S. economy slowly ascended from the depths of the Great Depression, a new world crisis emerged in 1939: World War II. Over the next year, it became increasingly apparent that the United States could not sit idly by as Great Britain fought the Germans.

Although the United States had not joined the conflict, war preparations were underway. The U.S. Congress in September 1940 passed the Selective Service Act calling for the first peacetime draft in American history. Close to 16 million American men between the ages of 21 and 36 were required to register at one of 6,500 draft boards across the country. Nearly 50 million men would register during the war.

Detroit manufacturers, some reluctantly, answered President Franklin D. Roosevelt's call in 1940 to supply munitions in the fight against the totalitarian threats of Nazi Germany and Imperial Japan.[1] Within a year, Detroit was building trucks, tanks and aircraft for the Allied forces and had become the symbol of the Arsenal of Democracy. By the war's end in 1945, Detroit was producing 25 percent of the war material built in the United States.[2]

The Calm Before the Storm

With America joining the war, the NRPCA balanced its traditional focus on programs, activities and advocacy with the pressing need to inform and involve Park residents in the war efforts. Programs and activities continued unabated. In September 1940, the second North Rosedale Park Fair and homecoming was held. Seeing the large crowds prompted an enthusiastic chairperson Fred Thomson to say: "We start off where the Michigan Fair left off. There will be blue ribbons galore."

The first Ice Carnival in January 1941 drew more than 500 individuals and featured ice skating exhibitions, races and barrel jumping, with prizes awarded for the most original costume. The next year, the Rosedale Park Woman's Club held what was believed to be its first Halloween event, Witches Wiggle Halloween Masquerade and Hard Times Party. Prizes were awarded for the most amusing, the tackiest, and most original costumes. In keeping with the wartime conservation program, attendees were encouraged to devise costumes of whatever they had on hand. A few years later, the Club sponsored a Halloween party for boys and girls to replace the practice of "begging" as it was called then. The October 1946 event drew 1500 children.

But NRPCA was more than just a social organization. It joined efforts to oppose plans for a new Detroit City Airport in the Eight Mile and Wyoming area. Following a report by a commission appointed by Mayor Edward Jeffries in favor of the plan, the matter went to City Council for consideration. The airport was never built.

On August 6, 1942, NRPCA president Leland Place called a meeting to create an organization of local associations to handle problems affecting the entire area. The Federated Civic Associations of Northwest Detroit was formed and included the Ardmore, Birwood Park, Brightmoor, Brookline, Evergreen Houghton, Grandmont, Lorland, Mayfair, Myland, Rosedale Park and North Rosedale Park organizations. The group grew to include 18 associations with plans to focus on housing, transportation, sanitation, taxation, building restrictions and other matters.

In November 1944, it filed a petition to stop the construction of an incinerator on Southfield Road near Fullerton to burn garbage. The group lost that battle, and the incinerator was eventually built. The next year, its board endorsed the City Planning Commission's program to convert the Redford golf course for summer use and for skating and other recreational sports. A plan proposed by the group the following year to speed up traffic on Grand River by using large new buses, limiting cars, and forbidding parking during rush hours was accepted by the Detroit Department of Street Railways (DSR).

Speeding and reckless driving were big problems in the Park, which led the NRPCA to form a traffic committee to study ways to discourage speeding. Sixty members signed a pledge to not drive over 25 mph in the area. Signs were installed around the neighborhood encouraging residents to report those who violated the traffic laws. At the Association's request, a traffic light was installed at McNichols and Outer Drive, the scene of numerous accidents, after complaints from nearby residents.

In the ongoing battle over tax assessments, the Association once again prevailed in a tax appeal with the City of Detroit in May 1944. The City had placed an assessment of $50,000 on the Community House and park, but the City Council voted to continue the exemption.

That December, the Association rolled out a plan to ask residents to surrender their certificates of indebtedness as a donation to the Association and the North Rosedale Park area. In 1938-39, residents had made loans to the Association to construct the new Community House. The Association planned to use the funds to retire the debt, make improvements to the Community House and surrounding land, and purchase equipment and building furnishings. The group also planned to purchase six lots (parcels 1806-1811) west of the Community House to expand the park. By June 1945, the amount donated stood at $14,925, nearly 80% of the certificates held by North Rosedale Park families.

NORTH ROSEDALE PARK CIVIC ASSOCIATION

Incorporated under the laws of the
State of Michigan

No. 401 $25.00

Certificate of Indebtedness

This is to certify that the NORTH ROSEDALE PARK CIVIC ASSOCIATION, a non-profit corporation duly organized under and by virtue of the laws of the State of Michigan, is indebted to:

Frank J. Noon — 16196 Shaftsbury — Detroit Michigan

in the sum of TWENTY-FIVE ($25.00) DOLLARS, for value received, which sum the North Rosedale Park Civic Association hereby promises to pay on the first day in July, in the year 1949, without interest, at its office in the City of Detroit, on the presentation and surrender of this certificate.

This certificate is one of a series of certificates amounting in the aggregate to Twenty-five Thousand ($25,000.00) Dollars, all of like tenor and effect.

The NORTH ROSEDALE PARK CIVIC ASSOCIATION shall and will apply the net proceeds of the sale of Lots 3705, 3706, 3707, 3708, 3709 and 3711, Rosedale Park Subdivision No. 13, Detroit, Michigan, to the payment pro rata of all outstanding certificates of indebtedness, aggregating said Twenty-five Thousand ($25,000.00) Dollars.

The maker hereof shall have the right of prepayment, in whole or in part, at any time.

This certificate is not assignable. The mailing of a check, in whole or part payment to the last known address of the holder shall discharge the maker pro tanto.

IN WITNESS WHEREOF, the NORTH ROSEDALE PARK CIVIC ASSOCIATION has caused this Certificate of Indebtedness to be signed by its President and its Secretary, and its corporate seal to be hereto affixed, at the City of Detroit, on the 5th day of October A. D. 1939.

Secretary — President

Members returned certificates of indebtedness and donated funds to the Civic Association

It's All Too Familiar

Then as now, the North Rosedale Park Civic Association, the Community House and its activities were primarily sustained by memberships and proceeds from events. Memberships fluctuated due to issues with employment, residents serving in the armed services, and just the uncertainty of the times. After hovering in the 300s for many years, a major membership drive was launched in November 1940. The young men from the local Boy Scout and Cub Scout troops and local high schools sought improvements to the skating rink and baseball diamond, which gave membership chairman Lester Deeley an idea. How about a membership contest with the young men competing to increase the number of members to cover the improvements they sought?

The young men were divided into six teams with a goal of soliciting 200 new members to cover the cost of creating two skating rinks; building a shelter for changing skates, checking shoes and keeping warm; and grooming the baseball diamond. Their efforts yielded 100 new members the first month and 174 new members in total.

Many of the problems that Park residents face today are some of the same challenges faced by residents 70, 80 and 90 years ago. Even then, individuals submitted Tattler articles after the deadline; residents complained of not receiving the newsletter; there were the ever present deviant youth; some residents wouldn't get involved in the neighborhood and didn't see the benefit of the Association; and there were complaints of speeding cars, racing motors, horns blowing after midnight, and loose dogs.

High on the list of issues plaguing the Park continued to be vandalism, and the youth of North Rosedale just wouldn't let up. In several 1941 Tattler articles, the editor expressed his frustration regarding broken windows at Cooke School; damage to the inside of the building; destruction of the ice and shelter at the rink; and broken streetlight bulbs. "One way to stop the unnecessary expense and inconvenience to the taxpayer and school authorities would be for parents to 'check up' on the activities of their children. If they possess BB guns, put them 'under wraps' as there exists a law against using them within the city limits. This disgraceful situation demands the attention of fathers and mothers in this section."

Individuals were admonished about placing rubbish in vacant lots (illegal dumping today). At times, the posts were intriguing. In November, *Tattler* editor Heber Hudson issued a notice to Glastonbury residents that a local dry cleaner had mistakenly delivered a dress to the wrong residence. Since the package did not have any information on who delivered the dress, the resident with the dress was asked to call the editor.

The Association began mailing the *Rosedale Tattler* to residents in the fall of 1943 rather than hand delivery.

Membership Numbers

1941 · **530 members**

1943 · **476 members**

1944 · **600 members**

1945 · **700 members**

1946 · **685 members**

1949 · **700 members**

The War, the War, the War

The Japanese attack on Pearl Harbor on December 7, 1941 forced the United States to declare war on Japan the next day, and the war being waged in

Europe and Asia came to American soil. By then, war production had begun to take its toll on businesses across the country. Floyd Odlum, a lawyer and industrialist, estimated that 20,000 small businesses might have to close because of the national defense program since an estimated 70 percent were not benefiting from the war boom.[3] A North Rosedale Park resident advertised for a job in the *Tattler* since his former job wasn't associated with the war effort.

While Park residents continued with normal activities as much as possible, supporting American troops was a top priority. For much of the 1940s, North Rosedale Park and its residents were front and center, from serving as American Red Cross volunteers to rationing materials to honoring service men and women. Use of the Community House as headquarters for air raid sector wardens, as well as for classes in first aid, home nursing, bandage making and home repairs, necessitated repeated requests for an increase in the Association's fuel oil allotment.

Responding to an appeal by the American Red Cross for volunteers, the Woman's Club raised funds for military personnel and their families; prepared surgical dressings; packed convalescent kit bags with writing materials, gum, cigarettes, cards, razors, soap and sewing kits; collected clothing for refugee children; and supplied food and services for members of the armed forces at the USO Canteen at Lafayette and Cass avenues. Members canvassed homes to collect for the 1943 War Chest Fund. The students at Cooke School also got in on the action and sold $259,625 in bonds during a drive in the spring of 1944.

The dedication of the Northwest aviation recruiting hangar on August 30, 1942 at Southfield, Grand River and Fenkell avenues drew a large enthusiastic crowd of military officials, air raid wardens, and local residents. The crowd buzzed with excitement at the sight and sound of a military flyover.

Conservation and rationing were other ways that Park residents contributed to the war effort. Residents were encouraged to salvage tin cans, grease, paper, rags, metals and rubber, all collected by area Girl Scouts. The Campfire Girls collected dishes, cups, plates and silverware for use in Red Cross canteens, expanded later to

Sales Tell Success Story

Free Press Photo

Mrs. Carl O. Ericke (left) joins Mrs. Pierre M. Mols in discussing the success of their ticket sales for the benefit dessert bridge the Rosedale Woman's Club is sponsoring at 1 p. m. Friday, Oct. 27. Funds are to be used to furnish hospital rooms for veterans.

The Woman's Club raises funds to furnish hospital rooms for veterans, *Detroit Free Press*

include stamps for the glue, and wastepaper.

In anticipation of gas rationing, the Association sought individuals who would be willing to swap rides as a way of saving gas and to avoid traveling crowded streets. Residents were encouraged to create Victory Gardens on vacant lots to help them supplement their rations with vegetables and fruit. Many grew flowers and planted trees as well.

Since many items were not available for purchase, the Association advertised for a refrigerator to rent. It would take two years before a new refrigerator arrived, courtesy of the bowling league.

Just like in the 1930s during the Great Depression, house construction was limited to $6000 as raw materials were diverted to the war effort, and new homes were smaller compared to homes built earlier.

Defense of the Country Hits Home

In March 1942, more than 500 North Rosedale Park residents attended a meeting to hear Glen Richards talk about civil defense and to view a film instructing civilians on how to fight incendiary bombs and be prepared for wartime emergencies.

The Office of Civilian Defense helped to organize the Air Raid Warden Service in anticipation that Detroit, as the Arsenal of Democracy, could become a bombing target. Through the effort, Detroit trained 9000 residents as air wardens to guard against air raids. North Rosedale Park, with its 80 blocks, had 150 wardens assigned to specific blocks. The wardens played an important role in blackout tests, which required every household to shut off all electricity. As part of the testing program, the Association encouraged blocks to get organized.

Mrs. C.W. Robinson remembered being a young woman during the darker days of World War II and going to the Community House to perform Red Cross volunteer work. She prepared bandages and served as an air raid warden. "I would go up and down the street and make sure everyone stayed inside ... not even a dog could be outside."

A total of 55 young men in the Rosedale Park area also signed up to become aviation cadets and eventually became members of the U.S. Army Air Corps.

George Tait of The Manufacturers National Bank of Detroit published the *Round Robin*, a series of newsletters from 1943-1946 sent to North Rosedale Park men serving in the war. Each issue highlighted letters from the "Round Robin Boys" as Tait called them, listed addresses, reviewed the latest standings of sports teams, told jokes, and provided updates on deposits toward a "hoped-for" Round Robin hunting lodge ($1870 collected by the end of the war). Pvt. Judy Ann McClain's letter in the second issue sought inclusion in what was

The Round Robin newsletter for military personnel

clearly a "men's only" club: "After reading several issues of 'The Round Robin,' which is a secret as to how they came into my possession, I have become ***very interested*** in joining your Group. My name is Judy Ann McClain, and I am a WAC in Uncle Sam's Army. I realize I would be the only female member, but please give my application some consideration ..."

As a tangible reminder of the service of Park residents, the NRPCA created a memorial in 1942, which included a banner composed of the U.S. flag and a list of residents with the years and fields of service, military branch, rank, promotions and any distinctions. Within a year, 194 names of Park residents were inscribed on the Armed Forces honor roll, which included a number of sets of brothers. By the war's end, there were 395 names, 14 with gold stars representing casualties of war.

In some cases, families made extreme sacrifices, sending two, three or even four sons off to war. That was the case with Mr. & Mrs. Gordon Brown. A February 1946 *Tattler* article talked about three of their sons – Sgt. Alan Brown, Pvt. Donald Brown and Capt. Kenneth Brown – all returning from service to the United States. A fourth son, Lt. Gordon Brown, a bombardier and Navigator, was the first Park resident killed in battle on February 4, 1943.

V-E Day (Victory in Europe) was declared on May 9, 1945 after Germany's surrender, followed by Japan's surrender on August 15 after the bombing of Hiroshima and Nagasaki. Expressing the sentiments of so many, Association president Andrew Pringle exclaimed, "The war is over! North Rosedale Park Civic Association gives thanks to those sons and

North Rosedale honors residents who served during World War II, November 1945

daughters of residents who served so that we might enjoy the peace we have today. To those who will not return from the wars, the residents owe more than can be described. To those brave boys we humbly give thanks. Their supreme sacrifice has made it possible for us to carry on as an organized community." *Rosedale Tattler*, September 1945

Trouble on the Homefront

As Detroit manufacturers ramped up war production, thousands and thousands of workers were needed. Women joined the workforce, taking on men's roles as men left for overseas to fight. African Americans also flocked to Detroit but were met by stiff resistance from whites who didn't want them in their neighborhoods or working next to them on assembly lines. In the 1940s, 80 percent of Detroit property outside of the inner city was subject to racial covenants, and white residents established neighborhood associations to enforce them.[4] Many Blacks were forced to live in substandard conditions in areas like Paradise Valley or confined to the Brewster Projects on Detroit's lower east side.

Humiliation and resentment on the part of whites and Blacks spilled over into the streets, so that by the early 1940s, racially-motivated street fights were common.[5] Eventually those feelings led to racial trouble on Detroit's northeast side, a precursor to the Detroit race riot in 1943.

To address the housing crisis, Sojourner Truth, a federal housing project, was built in northeast Detroit in a white section of the city. White protesters gathered to prevent Blacks from moving in, which earlier had ended in rioting. In February 1942, guarded by more than 1,500 State troopers and Detroit police, moving vans carried the families and their belongings into the complex.

The situation at Sojourner Truth was only the beginning. On June 20, 1943, more than 200 Black and white individuals fought on Belle Isle. Though police ended the violence by midnight, tensions soared and, later that night, two rumors led to malicious actions from both sides. African Americans, acting on a rumor that whites had thrown a Black woman and her baby off the Belle Isle Bridge, formed a mob and moved near Woodward Avenue, breaking windows, looting white businesses and attacking white individuals.

Nearby, angry whites, believing a rumor that Black men had raped a white woman near the same bridge, formed a mob and attacked Black men as they exited a theatre. As word of both incidents spread, so did the violence, which lasted for three days. It took Mayor Edward J. Jeffries asking President Franklin Roosevelt to deploy national troops before the violence was quelled. The result: Detroit race riots left 34 dead and hundreds injured.

It was against this backdrop that the North Rosedale Park Civic Association began its efforts to keep the Park the way it was.

The Issue of Race Comes to the Park

The NRPCA petitioned the Detroit City Council to change the zoning on the west side of Southfield Road and on the east side of Evergreen through North Rosedale Park from District R2 that allowed two-family homes to District R1 for single-family homes. The goal was to discourage the building of two-family homes on Southfield and Evergreen and to create consistency throughout the park. The move was in advance of restrictions in the area expiring in 1950. The rezoning was approved by the Council in early 1944.

The November 1943 *Tattler* contained the first reference to plans to squelch any possibility of bi-racial housing coming to the Park. The method to prevent that was the renewal of deed restrictions set to expire in 1950, which limited construction to single-family homes and only allowed individuals of the Caucasian race to live in North Rosedale. "Any community not protected by rigid restrictions would have no legal means of preserving its character and might soon become undesirable in the opinion of both residents and prospective purchasers."

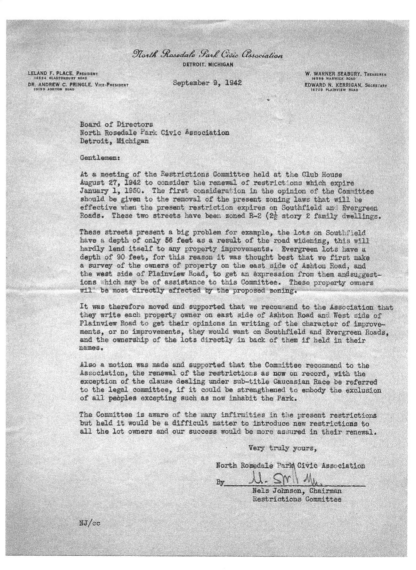

Over the next several years, Association leaders advocated for the renewal of the deed restrictions. However, it wasn't until December 1945 that the Association began soliciting residents' signatures to renew the restrictions prior to their expiration. In the Park, there were roughly 2000 parcels of land – 500 were for business purposes, 500 were vacant and another 1000 were private homes. The renewal required the signature of every individual who owned or had an interest in each and every piece of land in North

Unless otherwise above provided, all of the aforesaid terms, covenants, conditions, and restrictions shall be operative and in force until January 1st, 1950.
CAUCASIAN RACE: III.
This deed is given and accepted upon the express condition that neither the whole nor any part of the premises above described, nor the whole nor any part of any building or structure erected, or which may be erected thereon, shall at any time be sold or leased to or occupied by any person or persons other than those of the Caucasian Race.
EASEMENT. IV.

A paragraph from a deed for a North Rosedale Park home

Rosedale. The restrictions extension agreement form was even included in the *Tattler*. By November 1949, the Association still needed 311 more signatures. Even though the United States Supreme Court had ruled in 1947 that racially restrictive covenants violated the Equal Protection Clause of the Constitution, that didn't stop Association leaders from seeking renewal of the restrictions, which were now illegal.

Underlying the restrictions issue was prejudice against those who weren't Caucasian. At times, that prejudice was out in the open. As was common during that time, individuals often performed in black face. Such was the case at the June 1947 *Rosedale Jamboree*, North Rosedale's own minstrel show, including a performance of *Ol' Man River*. A picture of the cast mostly in black face was included in the July 1947 *Tattler* with the caption: "The two white men were C.R. Richards and C.H. Buckmaster. The rest all look alike."

As the war was winding down, the Association was dealing with typical neighborhood issues. Rats were the focus in April 1945. It was reported that 14 people in the city had been bitten by rats since January, and one person had infectious jaundice. It was estimated that there were three million rats in the city at the time.

Once again, the City assessed the NRPCA $68,000 for the Community House and parkland. In 1945, the assessment was appealed, and the City Council voted that the NRPCA was a service agency and therefore did not have to pay property taxes. The situation was resolved once again, for the moment.

The Rosedale Park Improvement Association published *The Rosedale Echo* in the 1930s, but it disappeared for some years. In 1946, the association restarted its newspaper as *The Rosedale Park News*. South Rosedale (as it was called then) had caught up to its neighbors to the north.

Yet, in terms of bowling, Rosedale Park was out in front. For a number of years, North

Rosedale and South Rosedale bowlers engaged in a battle. In January 1946, South had the edge on North four championships to two. By April, the score was six wins for South and four for North.

The Association hired private police protection to watch cars parked at the Community House for Civic Association meetings and other events in November 1946. The vandals were at it again!

An article in that same issue focused on new cement sidewalks replacing the temporary wooden blocks around the Community House. Apparently, the Association's earlier appeal to the City's Commissioner of Public Works for upgrades to address hazardous conditions from rotting planking on Glastonbury, Rosemont and Ashton had had an effect.

You've Come a Long Way, Baby!

There was a lot going on in and around the Park in 1947. The women of North Rosedale had formed a women's bowling league beginning with 36 bowlers at Grandmont Recreation. In celebration of completing the first year, the names of the bowlers, excluding the names of their husbands, were listed in the *Tattler*. By 1949, the league had its own *Tattler* article including scores and standings, maybe a first for the newspaper.

In July, Redford High School had its largest graduating class of 500 students including 42 residents from North Rosedale Park, with the graduation held in the Cooley High School auditorium. By August, construction had begun on a new addition to the school to connect the old and new buildings on three floors, and include administrative offices, a library with conference rooms, new classrooms, and teachers' study.

The conversion of the EVergreen telephone exchange to the KEnwood 2 exchange was announced in July 1947 to allow expansion, direct dial service to the suburbs, and operators to dial long-distance numbers in other cities. As a result, residents had to scramble to revise directories and phone books and learn new numbers.

New shelter at Community House dedicated June Day 1948

October 1947 saw the launch of the campaign for the Community Chest of Metropolitan Detroit – the precursor to United Way of Southeastern Michigan – to benefit 125 Red Feather services across the area. The campaign involved six radio stations broadcasting the campaign kick-off from Grand Circus Park – the first time that all the stations carried the same program. The organization recruited one woman per block to cover all 12,000 blocks in Detroit to solicit funds for the effort. The goal for the year was $5.35 million.

That same year, the Association made plans to sell vacant lots on Lancashire to pay off the remaining bond obligations on the Community House; formed The Boys Club of North Rosedale Park for boys aged 14-18; and started the North Rosedale Park Glee Club with 20

NRPCA's 25th anniversary celebration, October 9, 1948

members, most of whom were participants from the earlier minstrel show.

On June Day 1948, the NRPCA dedicated a new shelter with additional storage for Association property as well as enlargement of the parking area to allow for more parking on site and not on the street.

The year of 1948 was a milestone as the Woman's Club and the Civic Association both celebrated 25th anniversaries. The Woman's Club celebration on October 20 drew 313 members and 33 guests and included a dramatic presentation of the Club's history involving skits, music and photographs.

The Association's October 9 celebration began with a special membership meeting that included vignettes depicting significant periods in the history of North Rosedale Park, a movie on the Park's history, the unveiling of a new North Rosedale song, and men's chorus performance. The event drew the largest all-male crowd – more than 400 – in the Association's history.

For the occasion, Henry Morton composed "Ode to North Rosedale Park."

So to Rosedale Park I'm singing -
Oh we're jolly and we're happy and we're free.
To our Rosedale Park I'm clinging
Cause we're neighborly and friendly, can't you see?
So let's raise our voices merrily
For it's here we make friends and want to be
Ever loyal to our friends so true,
The U.S.A. and our city, too;
'Cause we love them all as you do too;
North Rosedale Park for me!

Tattler Editor J. Harold Stevens in 1948 noted, "One might well ask what our community would be like had there not been a strong and active organization to guard its collective interests. Who would have won the boulevard cases, enforced the restrictions, provided two community buildings, playgrounds and ice rinks? Who would have provided a community news magazine just for North Rosedale Park? Who would have provided for June Day, an ice carnival and activities for the children, so popular in the Park? If there were no Civic Association, would North Rosedale be considered the ideal neighborhood of Detroit?"

Bill Hudson and Jack Lillie chronicled 25 years of history in North Rosedale Park

Mayor Albert Cobo

The *Tattler* had a different look that year as new graphics, courtesy of William Coppock of Ashton Street, were included in the publication. Coppock, a commercial artist, donated his time to promote the NRPCA's expansion fund efforts. By this time, large portions of *Tattlers* were devoted to announcements of engagements, weddings, and now births, an indication that the Baby Boom was underway. The exploding birth rate in the United States – more than 65 million were born from 1941-1961 – was attributed to veterans returning from the war, the strong post-war economy and pop culture that idealized parenthood and large families. [6]

Albert Cobo had moved to the Park sometime in 1947 or 1948 and spoke at the Association's meeting in June 1949. He declared his candidacy the very next month and was elected mayor in November. In a special statement in the *Rosedale Tattler* after his election, Cobo said, "Tell the people of North Rosedale Park that I appreciate their almost unanimous support, and that they will have the kind of government they want; efficient, courageous, economical and in the best interests of all of the people of Detroit."

In addition to Mayor Cobo, Rosedale Park (both North and South) boasted of a number of officials as residents. They included George Boos, Lancashire, Police Commissioner; William Rogell, South Rosedale, City Council; and Harry Durbin, housing director. Rosedale Park was well represented in City government.

As the decade ended, the NRPCA was experiencing financial challenges – the rising cost of operating the Community

House and the need to increase income, since membership dues were not enough to cover expenses. In contention was the fact that groups were not charged to use the Community House. A subcommittee was formed to address the Association's financial shortfall. In light of these challenges, the Woman's Club decided to hold a benefit party to replenish necessary kitchen equipment. The members acknowledged that, despite using the facilities for ten years, they had provided very little financial support.

Post War dinner celebration, December 1945

DR. "ANDY" PRINGLE. president of the Civic association and ardent June day worker, was drafted as grand marshal of the June day parade. "Doc" could not delegate the job because no one else available could ride the horse.

June Day 1945

18425 Bretton, constructed with concrete and steel, was listed as a Detroit bomb shelter during the Cold War

THE 1950S

After World War II, the 1950s ushered in the golden age. As people were able to find jobs with ease, Americans rushed out to buy cars, homes, appliances and the new thing – televisions. This was the Baby Boom era, as troops returned home wanting to get married and begin a family.

Locally, Detroit's mighty industrial engine was still going strong, with America's roads filled with cars built in the Motor City. Detroit's population peaked at almost 1.85 million, making it America's fourth-largest city. With 296,000 manufacturing jobs, Detroit, once again, saw an influx of people coming from across the country to gain employment with one of the Big Three auto companies: Ford, General Motors and Chrysler.[1]

Many suburbs popped up all around the Detroit area, housing the many people who worked in the automobile business. With the push to build the nation's highway system, fleeing to the suburbs for a different life became an increasingly more popular option. Whites, who could afford to, moved in droves throughout the late '50s and well into the '60s to escape traffic, crime and racial problems. Outright fear of Blacks and increased levels of racial tension only made the suburban life more attractive.[2]

We Like It Just the Way It Is

The possibility of integration was felt in North Rosedale Park. For a number of years, the Association had sought to renew restrictions to reserve the area for single-family homes and determine who could and could not live in the Park. Deed restrictions declared that only those of the Caucasian race could reside in North Rosedale Park. By February 1950, 92% of the property owners had signed to have the restrictions renewed, but the January 1 deadline had passed.

The Association came out in support of Detroit Mayor Albert Cobo's veto of the City Council's approval of a permit to construct a co-operative housing complex in the Telegraph and Schoolcraft area in 1950. His veto was upheld by a 5-3 Council vote. Cobo and the NRPCA were opposed to any multi-unit buildings in areas with single-family homes. In September, the NRPCA contributed $100 to aid the Tel-Craft Civic Association in its fight against the project.

The Restrictions Committee continued its work to ensure that building and zoning restrictions were followed in the Park. The Association and affected residents banded together to oppose a petition by the A&P store to rezone property on Bretton Drive in back of its store to construct a parking lot. The City Planning Commission agreed with the subdivision and denied the petitioner's request.

Keeping Residents Safe

In the early 1950s, safety was on the minds of City officials and a coalition of organizations led by the Traffic Safety Association of Detroit and the Detroit Police Department. The Traffic Safety Association, Police Department and its partners launched a comprehensive program in 1950 to promote driver and pedestrian safety. They began by distributing agreements for fathers and their teen children to sign, pledging to observe safe driving practices. Bright neon 'Walk, Don't Walk' signals were installed by the City in 32 locations, mostly at school crossings.

That summer, the association distributed stickers to remind children and their parents on how to cross a street safely. Those of a certain age may remember this: STOP at the curb; LOOK both ways; WAIT until it's safe; then WALK across the street. With the start of school, the organization did a media blitz that included billboards, posters, newspaper articles, ads, leaflets, television programs and other media with the theme, Watch Out for Kids!

Detroit's traffic safety program received a first-place award in 1954 from the National Safety Council for outstanding achievement in both public safety education and safety organization.

As has been the case off and on over the years, North Rosedale Park employed a private patrol service financially supported by residents. Yet, even in the '50s, it was hard to get individuals to pay. "It is, in my opinion, this type of surveillance ... which makes it possible for residents of North Rosedale to have a minimum of fear of the burglarizing, prowling, assaulting, and other types of crimes being committed in other neighborhoods of our city. I have been in-

Poster from Traffic Safety Association campaign, 1952

formed, however, that there are only a few people in the park willing to see that this service is continued for the betterment of our neighborhood ... I would and do encourage each and every one of you to contact Mr. Ward, and see what arrangements you can make with him so as we may all benefit and retain his services." Signed, Your Neighbor

The Ever-Changing *Tattler*

The *Tattlers* in the 1950s had more photos and shorter stories than previous issues. The July 1950 issue included photos from the June Day event and Girl Scout and Brownie troops' activities.

In December 1951, J. Harold Stevens retired as the editor of the *Rosedale Tattler* after 14 years. George A. Harding, an experienced journalist and editor, took over. Harding began using women's first names in the *Tattlers*, but just as quickly as their names appeared, those in subsequent issues slipped back to the old ways.

While most articles were from the editor or contributors, occasionally a letter to the editor got readers' attention. A resident in 1950 wrote: "My gripes are because of the gripes I hear. Whenever I hear a fault-finder, I am first tempted to look in the list of association members to see if that family is represented in its roster. Usually it is not. But sometimes I find the name listed and further investigation shows little constructive activity on the part of that person. The general attitude seems to be 'let George (or Lacy) do it.' Sometimes the gripe is because some committee chairman hasn't done all the complainer thought he should do. The question arises what did you do about it? ... But by and large, we have a wonderful community and a grand civic association and every officer and every committee chairman deserves consideration, help, and praise."

While some residents appreciated the work of the Association, others didn't see its value. One member expressed his concerns. What is the association doing outside of social functions? Association President Albert Finly responded by listing a number of items: maintenance of a skating rink; summer recreation program for children; June Day; placement of safety signs; checking on building restrictions for new homes; liaison with the police department; recommendations for the Southfield Expressway; traffic and safety suggestions to the City of Detroit; publishing the monthly newsletter; and keeping the grounds and the Community House in good shape for groups to meet and events to take place.

The writer also suggested that the organization was dormant. Finly's response: "May I suggest that instead of firing a shot gun you let go with a rifle and tell us specifically in what direction we are taking action that will {not} benefit the entire neighborhood. It is comprised of voluntary workers, voluntary officers, voluntary committees and committee members –

all serving without pay – in addition to their full-time business and family lives. But a total of 300 officers and committee members right now in 1958 can vigorously testify that it is a long way from being 'dormant.' "

It was rather puzzling why *Tattler* editors published (or residents submitted) information about upcoming vacation plans. In September 1951, the *Tattler* began publishing information on residents' travel after returning home. After one too many break-ins, someone finally got wise.

Theatre Comes to the Park

In May 1951, the Association decided to put on *Holiday Escapades*, a musical revue to benefit the Community House expansion fund. The show made history as females were included in a Civic Association show for the first time. *Bells-A-Hoppin* followed in 1952, which included actors in black face. The next year, the Association presented *Sing Out, Sweet Land*, a musical biography of American songs from the days of the Puritans to the present.

Building on the success of its theatrical productions, the Association created the Park Players on June 15, 1953. The theatre group presented its first performance – three, one-act plays – in December. Tickets were only $1.

The November 1955 *Tattler* featured Backstage with the Park Players, the first column to inform residents of the troupe's activities. The group put on its first musical production, *Wild Rose*, which many called "the best show ever put on in Rosedale Park." The success of *Time of the Cuckoo* allowed Park Players to install $760 of lighting equipment in the Community House, including a control panel, and border and floodlights.

Each year, and sometimes twice a year, Park Players put on a theatrical production. In 1958, it was the children's turn. The lights were on. The stage was set. The young actors took their places. The theater troupe of 48 Park children – divided into two performances – truly broke some legs in *Aladdin and the Wonderful Lamp*. After the young thespians' perfor-

Park Players' first performance in 1953

mance, one member of Park Players remarked, "We could be replaced, you know."

Park Players went on to become one of Michigan's oldest community theatre organizations.

The Park and the City

Mayor Cobo and Detroit Department of Street Railways (DSR) Commissioner Herman Moekle, both North Rosedale Park residents, participated in a ceremony in August 1950 placing the first trolley pole for electric buses scheduled to operate on Grand River. Moekle also was credited with ending the DSR strike the following year.

Louis Schrenk, chairman of the NRPCA traffic committee, served as superintendent of the Public Lighting Commission. A heating plant run by the Lighting Commission was named in his honor in 1953, the same year Mayor Cobo was re-elected for a third term.

By the mid-fifties, thanks to City Council and Mayor Cobo, Rosedale Park residents saw a reduction on average of $7 per front foot in property assessments. For the first time, Civic Association representatives were allowed to contest assessments on behalf of all property owners in the area. Cobo also was credited with a $54-million water works program to supply water to 43 communities, and $68 million to improve the sewer system to prevent flooded streets and basements.

Under Cobo's leadership, the City continued to expand its transportation options as the first major freeway construction began with the John C. Lodge and the Edsel Ford freeways. Ten-year projects, both were built jointly by the State of Michigan, Wayne County, the City of Detroit and the federal government. The first sections of the Lodge Freeway ran 3.6 miles from Pallister to Jefferson. The Ford Freeway extended 5.5 miles from Wyoming to John R.

Lodge Freeway construction
© Michigan Department of Transportation

Historians believe the freeways were a double-edged sword. "Instead of making the city more accessible and bringing folks in, it caused the city to bleed out, both population and businesses. The freeways simply made it easier for folks to live elsewhere – where yards were bigger, homes were newer and property was cheaper – yet still work downtown."[3]

Known to play up racial tensions, Mayor Cobo was seen as an ally by some for his opposition to the expansion of public housing for Blacks, especially into white neighborhoods, in an attempt to protect whites' property values. Yet for Blacks, he was an adversary. He was blamed for not addressing housing discrimination and for pushing for freeways that demolished the center of Black life in Detroit – Paradise Valley and the Black Bottom. After erasing these neighborhoods from existence starting in 1950, the land would sit unused and overgrown for some five years. "Black Detroiters watched their community flattened for an overgrown wasteland of nothingness."[4]

A convention center was the vision of several Detroit mayors dating back as far as Hazen Pingree in the 1890s. However, Mayor Cobo managed to move it from concept to reality, creating a center that was an integral part of downtown Detroit. Construction of the $56-million center, a sprawling complex on Detroit's riverfront, took four years and was completed in 1960. The center was named after Mayor Cobo, who died in 1957 before its completion.

The decade also saw construction of Ford Auditorium and the City-County Building, a new office building for City of Detroit and Wayne County offices and local courts. In 1958, the Spirit of Detroit, a statue designed by famed sculptor Marshall Fredericks, was dedicated, quickly becoming Detroit's most significant icon.

To address the need for police protection in the rapidly growing northwest section of Detroit, a new police precinct was built at 21400 Grand River at McNichols. The 16th Precinct, which later became the 8th Precinct, was officially dedicated on October 13, 1955. The building was eventually demolished in 2014, and a new building dedicated across the street in 2017.

Martha Griffiths, a member of the Michigan State Legislature from 1949-52, became the first woman to address the Civic Association in 1953. She spoke about her support of the proposal by Michigan Governor G. Mennen Williams to institute a corporate income tax to address the State's deficit. Griffiths and her husband, Hicks, both attorneys, lived on Warwick Street in North Rosedale.

Civic Association Grows, Activities Expand

The Civic Association saw its largest increase in members in the 1950s. By 1951, the membership dues were still $10, and the Association had nearly 800 members. In 1955, the Association launched a major membership drive with the slogan, "105 for 1005 in 55," meaning 105 new members for a total membership of 1005 in 1955. The initiative resulted in 1042 members, an all-time high.

Association membership badge worn on men's lapels

At the Association's annual election meeting and Past Presidents Night in January 1953, 300 members showed up, making it the largest crowd in years. It was the first dinner meeting in the organization's history and a big reunion.

Not only were Association memberships on the rise, participation in June Day continued to increase. It was a banner year for the annual June Day event as 600 individuals joined the parade in 1955, making it the largest June Day in many years. The next year was even bigger with more than 800 parade participants.

Park children had more fun things to do as the Association started a summer recreation program in 1954, offering group games, crafts, softball, volleyball, basketball and other activities. A total of 159 kids participated in the seven-week program.

Believed to be the first event of its kind, the Association sponsored a Father-Daughter-Son event in September 1956. Entertainment was provided by Wayne Puppeteers directed by Fern Zwickey, an art professor at Wayne State University. This was followed by Family Nite, featuring a meal prepared free of charge by Harold and Violet Cregar, owners of Cregar's Pickwick House, a popular local restaurant. Cregar requested that all proceeds from donations be used to purchase dishwashing equipment for the Community House. The event drew a crowd of 425 and raised $844 for the Association.

Cregar's Pickwick House, Grand River and Outer Drive

The spirit of North Rosedale Park was on full display at Pioneer Night as more than 130 longtime residents, who had lived in the Park for 20 or more years, were honored in 1957. The room was filled with nostalgia as stories were told of the old wooden clubhouse and its famous potbelly stove; the days when homes were a block apart; and how people moved to get out of the smoke zone into the ozone.

> "The meeting was one of the best in the community's history and the events of the evening proved that these hearty pioneers properly laid the groundwork for the best civic association in the Detroit area and possibly the entire nation."
>
> GEORGE HARDING, *Tattler* Editor

With less cars on the street in those days and public transportation much to be desired, members recalled men adorning their cars with a medallion with a red rose. Any resident stranded downtown or waiting for the streetcar service was free to hail the driver to ask for a ride.

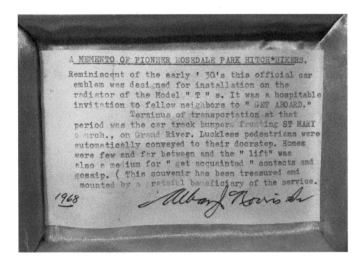

Explanation of Rosedale Park medallion

In Harry St. John's letter in 1957, he wrote: "Someone kindly sent me a copy of the May *Tattler*. It pleases me to no end to read of the Park's manifold activities and to learn from them what a living force exists in the community I helped to found. Please give my kindest regards to my many Rosedale friends who still live in what most certainly is one of America's finest suburban communities." St. John was a past Association president and the *Tattler's* first editor.

St. John's comments were echoed by outgoing NRPCA President Al Finly at a 1958 event honoring more than 300 volunteers who worked to enhance life in the Park: "This is Rosedale Park! North Rosedale Park cannot be defined by streets or boundaries. It is not houses or lawns or trees, as attractive as they may be. North Rosedale Park is people ... good neighbors who have banded together in a cooperative civic association to make living better for all the men, women and children of their community."

The Park and Its Schools

North Rosedale Park was known for its commitment to education and the number of educators living here. Charles Wolfe (16575 Huntington) was named principal of Redford

High School to fill the vacancy created by the death of Homer Clark. Wolfe was an assistant principal at Mumford High School and had been an employee of the Detroit Board of Education since 1937.

Other educators in the Park included Earl Laing, Detroit Public Schools District Principal; Dr. Paul Rankin, Detroit Public Schools Assistant Superintendent; Dr. Samuel Brownell, Detroit Public Schools Superintendent; Henry Eddy, Northeastern High School Principal; and Dr. David Henry, Wayne University President.

Eighth-grade graduation in new auditorium at Cooke School, 1953

Cooke School got a new auditorium, and graduation exercises for its 65 eighth-graders were held in it on June 15, 1953. Of the 65 students, 24 had attended Cooke from kindergarten through eighth grade.

Enrollment in Detroit Public Schools continued to increase. The total enrollment in 1953 was 251,881 compared to 240,081 the previous year, a 4.9 percent increase.

A highlight of the decade was the Tone Weavers, a choral group of Cooke School mothers. Founded in September 1952 by Marion Rice and comprised mostly of North Rosedale Park residents, the group performed throughout the 1950s at numerous church, school and organizational events. There was NRPCA's Ladies Night; Father's Night at Cooke School; a

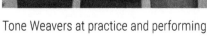

Tone Weavers at practice and performing

Good Friday program on WWJ-TV; a benefit bridge party at the Community House; Northwest YMCA groundbreaking; and Christmas music at Bushnell Church. Members were charged a $1 membership fee plus 50 cents a week. By the mid '50s, there were 23 members.

Woman's Club Shows Its Support

In April 1950, the Rosedale Park Woman's Club welcomed 47 new members to its ranks and presented $500 to the Association in June for the purchase of a new stove for the Community House. The Club hit a milestone two years later with 548 members, the largest membership of any women's club in the Detroit area.

The Woman's Club launched a new event: an artists' curb sale featuring an art exhibit and sale of paintings and ceramics created by Park children and adults. The event was a success with 358 entries – 210 pictures and 148 pieces of pottery.

The Woman's Club also celebrated its 30th anniversary in October 1953 with a tea and dramatic one-act play. Continuing an annual tradition, both the NRPCA and the Woman's Club held special nights for the opposite sex: Husband's Night for the Woman's Club, Ladies Night for the all-male NRPCA.

Woman's Club Curb Art Show, September 1953

When George Anderson, radio playwright and author of *How to Get More of Your Money* spoke to the Club in March 1958, he gave the audience a reason to smile. "People generally persist in clinging to the fallacy you can save money and get rich. High taxes and low interest rates have made such a possibility extremely remote if not completely impossible. You save money to spend. It shouldn't be a savings account but a spending account." Following the speech, the Woman's Club report was: "If you've noticed happy expressions on the faces of the ladies in Rosedale Park it is because they ... learned to have a spending account and not a savings account and that seemed to strike a happy chord." (*Tattler*, April 1958)

As demonstrated over the years, North Rosedale residents were generous with their time and finances in support of charitable causes. The NRPCA supported the United Foundation's Torch Drive campaign to raise funds for human service organizations. Detroit became the first major city to organize a fundraising drive within companies. From 1950-53, led by the Woman's Club, North Rosedale exceeded its annual goal.

As polio wreaked havoc in the lives of Detroiters and residents of North Rosedale Park, the women took part in an emergency March of Dimes event to raise funds to assist in providing medical care for the polio victims in the area. Numerous *Tattler* articles implored readers to make sure they received the Salk vaccine. Unfortunately, many residents simply ignored pleas from doctors. Detroit's polio epidemic in 1958, second only to the one in 1952, resulted in 649 cases, 346 of them resulting in paralysis and 23 deaths. The largest percentage of those cases, 91.6%, occurred in the central area of Detroit.[5]

Community House Improvements

The Community House got a fresh look in 1953 as walls were painted, draperies hung and furniture reupholstered in the lobby and ladies' powder room. The work was supervised by Dr. Don Kaump, Walter Bieneman and Holland Bus Weir.

To show off the improvements and to celebrate its 30th anniversary, the NRPCA invited residents to an open house. Outdoor improvements included a new asphalt driveway, 18 new shrubs, newly installed iron pipes to prevent motorists from driving over the lawn, and an outdoor drinking fountain. Inside, the kitchen was spruced up with new counters, garbage disposal, storage closet, new floor tiles and lighting. Second-floor balcony floors were retiled.

Answering the call for financial support, 300-plus residents contributed $9000 to an improvement fund for the building and park the following year.

While the Association directors and members worked tirelessly to improve the Community House, vandals were busy destroying it. Vandalism reached an alarming level, especially in October 1955 when the building was broken into eight times in two weeks. In 1955 alone, the Association had to replace some 200 window panes and stolen equipment. The Association spent an estimated $1500-$2000 each year to repair damage done by vandals.

According to Association President Milton Drake, "We have the names of seven boys who were responsible for or participated in the recent damage and illegal entry to the property. It is not our intention at this time to take any action until making this last appeal to the parents. However ... if the parents are unable to control their children, the Association intends to approach the Police Department for help and to prosecute offenders to the full extent permitted by the law."

Sometime in the fall of 1950, the Association closed the Community House parking lot entrance at Bretton Drive to stop motorists from using the parking lot for racing. That might explain why there's only one entrance to the parking lot.

An April 1956 *Tattler* article focused on the Dutch Elm disease that had destroyed thousands of elm trees in Detroit in the 1950s and some 1800 elm trees in 1955 alone. North Rosedale, known for its beautiful canopy of elm trees, lost many trees to the disease, although residents were encouraged to do their part to save them.

The Plan that Would Never End

At the request of the NRPCA, representatives of several civic and community organizations met for a public hearing on the Southfield Expressway project in March 1958. Emil Coolidge (Ashton) headed the Southfield Freeway committee for NRPCA and put forth a new proposal – add just one additional lane in both directions to the present highway. The proposal was turned over to the City, Wayne County and State Highway agencies for further study.

Public Works Commissioner Glenn Richard said, "The City planner, the City traffic engineers, City expressway engineer and I all agree that the interests of the property owners in the Southfield area can best be served by the improvements proposed in the new agreement."

The commission came up with yet another plan that included the complete depression of the highway at mile and half-mile roads for an additional $3.3 million. This plan would be within the existing right-of-way and would not affect any other property in the Park. Also in consideration was the closing of Puritan to through traffic on the west side of Southfield.

The compromise plan that was approved by City, County and State agencies in the fall of 1958 involved the highway retaining its present width of 204 feet, and underpasses constructed at the main intersections. No homes were to be condemned on the east side of Ashton.

Even Association leaders had a hard time keeping up with the project. "Each administration has a 'cross to bear' and mine in particular was the planning of the Southfield Expressway," said past NRPCA President Al Finly. "As I remember

Southfield Freeway under construction
© Michigan Department of Transportation

it, the administration of that year, 1958, was even called un-American in spite of the many demands we made on the City Council and other government officials for information on what was going to happen."

The decade ended on a high note with the creation of Motown Records by Berry Gordy in 1959. In the 1960s, the company captured the hearts of Americans with the sweet sounds of artists like the Supremes, the Temptations, Martha and the Vandellas, Marvin Gaye, Stevie Wonder, and the Jackson 5, and became a worldwide phenomenon.

Park Pioneer William Hudson and Mrs. Hudson pictured in the living room of their home on Huntington road. The Hudsons have been residents here since 1926. Bill is a former president of the Association and was the keynote speaker at the successful Pioneer's Program held in May. — (Photo courtesy E. Fredericks' of Diane's Studio of Photography.)

Teen Dance at the Community House, December 1952

THE 1960S

The 1950s seemed profoundly tranquil compared to the turbulent 1960s. The decade would be characterized by a challenge to societal norms – rebellion against authority; anti-war sentiments; the fight for civil rights; music evolution; sexual freedom; rising drug use; civil unrest; and assassinations. The 1960s could be considered the most volatile decade of the 20th Century.

Detroit exemplified two prominent themes of the decade – civil unrest and civil rights.

In the city, residents were putting pressure on the police department to crack down on crime. The tactics police used to carry out that crackdown helped to further drive a wedge in an already divided city.

"[The police] often stopped and frisked and harassed African-American men, particularly those who were driving through or walking through predominantly white sections of the city," said Thomas Sugrue, author of a book on race and inequality. "That created a lot of tension and it remained very much unresolved in 1967."[1]

What began with the Detroit Police Department raiding an illegal nightclub on 12th Street in a predominantly black neighborhood on July 23, 1967 soon led to five days of rioting. The racial unrest in Detroit was the nation's worst: 43 were killed, more than 1100 injured, 7000 arrested and 2500 buildings destroyed, and property damage in excess of $45 million. "There were riots all around – it wasn't just Detroit," said Detroiter William Pattinson. "You felt like, for the first time, this country isn't going to make it. It was the closest I ever felt that our government was going to fall apart."[2]

White flight to the suburbs, which had started decades earlier, intensified after the rebellion. Roughly 40,000 white people exited the city in 1967, and that number doubled again the next year. [3]

Although known for the riots, the city was also known for its work during the civil rights movement. As the African-American population grew, patterns of discrimination led to a massive economic and physical divide. Discriminatory housing practices steered Black people of all income levels into segregated neighborhoods. In response, organizations like the NAACP, CORE, and the Northern Student Movement advocated for auto workers and worked to change discriminatory employment and housing practices. That work was evident in June 1963 when Dr. Martin Luther King Jr. led the civil rights Freedom Parade down Woodward Avenue, which included many of Detroit's leaders in support of the cause.

While the fight for civil rights was being waged in Detroit, North Rosedale Park leaders were still fighting against it. Yet it was only a matter of time before African Americans would find their way to the Park. Even then, prejudice would die a very slow death.

Activism Rules the Day

There were 1257 homes in the Park by December 1960. Of that number, 925 men were Association members, roughly 74% of the households in the area. Its work was carried out by 38 subcommittees focused on many areas, including taxes, insurance, building and grounds, restrictions, parks and boulevards, recreation programs, traffic and safety, legal, membership and hospitality.

The Park's reputation for activism, especially in political affairs, was reflected in supporting Park residents running for public office, criticizing officials whose decisions it opposed, and taking a stand on many issues of the day. Association President Philip Gelbach criticized a ruling by the Securities and Exchange Commission prohibiting a broker or salesperson from refusing to perform any real estate service because of an individual's race, color, religion, national origin or ancestry. Gelbach, along with the members of the Federated Civic Association of Northwest Detroit, said similar legislation had been rejected earlier and the Commission should not decide such matters.

The Rosedale Park Republican Club was formed in 1959 to inform members on subjects pertaining to the Republi-

Detroit Mayor Jerome Cavanagh, Association meeting speaker, 1962

can Party. That led to Weldon Yeager, J. Harold Stevens, and James Sterrett, all Republicans, being elected to the Michigan State Constitutional Convention in 1961.

On one of its regularly sponsored Candidates' Nights, the Association tried to have its own gubernatorial debate with Michigan Governor John Swainson and challenger George Romney. Only Romney attended but "made a hit with his North Rosedale Park audience," noting the need for citizens to be more involved in political party activities. "We rely too much on government to do the job for us."

Newly elected Detroit Mayor Jerome Cavanagh was the speaker at the NRPCA meeting in March 1962. When he took office, he was the youngest person to serve as Detroit's mayor at age 33. Despite a tough race against incumbent Louis Miriani, Cavanagh won the election, drawing focus on Miriani's poor race relations with Detroit's African-American population.

By March 1961, the State Highway Commission had determined that the proposed Grand River Expressway (renamed the Jeffries Expressway) would not run through Rosedale Park along Grand River. While that matter was being settled, the plans for the Southfield Freeway were not. After years of discussions and negotiations, plans changed again when the State Highway Commission indicated it needed 255 to 275 feet as a buffer, which would require condemnation of lots on Ashton Street.

Two groups of residents on Ashton organized but with competing propositions. Caught in the middle, the Association decided to work with the residents and fight condemnation. The condemnation proposal was defeated.

Of special interest to the Association was a rezoning proposal to locate Biff's Grill restaurant on commercial property at Bretton Drive and Fenkell. To allow additional time to study the proposal, the Association asked the City Planning Commission to delay its recommendation to the City Council for a month. After working out an agreement on amendments to the proposal with restaurant owner Oliver Roemer, the Association dropped its opposition.

The next year, the restaurant owners requested a change to the zoning for a portion of property on lot 1613 to allow for straightening of the alleyway and gaining additional parking space. Once again, Association members sought a 30-day delay in the hearing before the Commission. Finally, in 1968, the restaurant owners offered to make several property improvements in return for the Association's support for non-conforming use of the land. Feeling it was the best possible settlement, the Association board approved the arrangement.

North Rosedale Park: Home of Leaders

So many distinguished and talented residents have called North Rosedale home over the years, including Fern Wagner, 16615 Rosemont. She was recognized by the National

Convention of United Federation of Doll Clubs in August 1960 for her collection of antique pedlar dolls, believed to be the largest in the country.

Dr. Richard Jaynes was a featured soloist with the Detroit Symphony Orchestra at a benefit concert for Providence Hospital in November 1961. Dr. Jaynes, who did his internship and residency in obstetrics at Providence, was a soloist with Rackham Chorus and the Westminster Presbyterian Church Choir.

Roman S. Gribbs, 16515 Edinborough, former Assistant Wayne County prosecutor, entered private practice before being appointed as a Traffic Court Referee and serving as Wayne County Sheriff. As the 1960s came to an end, North Rosedale Park could boast of having a neighbor at City Hall again. Gribbs was elected mayor in November 1969.

Other noted Rosedale residents included J. Harold Stevens of Huntington Road, delegate to the Michigan Constitutional Convention in the early 1960s and State Representative for the 17th District; Dr. Joseph Montante, a physician, 18715 Bretton Drive, State Representative for the 17th District; and Thomas Poindexter, 16780 Edinborough, who finished first in the nomination for the Detroit City Council, ultimately defeating Jackie Vaughn in the November election.

The Association suffered a great loss with the death of its president DeWitt "Dee" Severance, 53, of a heart attack in August 1962. For 25 years, Severance had lived in the Park and served as the funeral director at Severance Funeral Home, 19621 W. McNichols, as well as president of the Parents' Club of Redford High School and the Michigan Funeral Directors Association No. 1. In his tribute to Severance, Bill Stockwell said, "Dee Severance was the kind of man who makes a community better. He was a good friend, a good neighbor, a good citizen. I hope there will be a lot of Dee Severances in North Rosedale Park to follow in his footsteps." Stockwell was tapped to replace Severance as president.

Fifteen past presidents were honored with a plaque

Park Civic Leader, NRPCA Head, Dies

DEWITT C. SEVERANCE

North Rosedale Park lost one of its most outstanding citizens and civic leaders last month when death claimed NRPCA President DeWitt C. "Dee" Severance, 53, at his summer home on Whitmore Lake. He died suddenly of a heart attack on the morning of August 9.

Dee had been a resident of North Rosedale Park for the past 25 years and a funeral director at the Severance Funeral Home, 19621 W. McNichols, for the same number of years.

He was president of the Parents' Club of Redford High school at the time of his death. He was a past-president of the Strathmoor Lions club, the Northwest Exchange club,

and the Michigan Funeral Directors association No. 1. He was a member of the Moslem Shrine, Redford Lodge No. 152 F&AM, Northwestern Sportsmen's club, Redford Hi-12 club, and American Legion Post 390.

He was a native of Detroit and was a graduate of Southwestern high school.

For many years Dee presided over the cook tent at the annual June Day events held in North Rosedale Park, where he was especially popular with the children.

To compensate for his extremely busy life, the Severances enjoyed their retreat at Whitmore Lake and spent as much time as possible there during the warm weather.

(Continued on Page 2)

with their names, which was presented to President Stockwell at the Association's December 1963 meeting. The plaque was engraved with the names of the 27 presidents who served from 1924-1963. "Now I know what happens to past presidents. They cast them in bronze

North Rosedale Park Civic Association past presidents, 1963

and put them on a plaque," quipped Stockwell.

Jack Lillie, a former Association President, said, "This area is still one of the nicest places to live in Michigan. Also, please note that about 70 committeemen work each year, so in the past 40 years, 2800 jobs have been well done by them. This has always been the strength of our group. We don't 'let George do it' – we do it ourselves!"

The *Rosedale Tattler*

The *Tattler* took on a funny tone in February 1963 as Association President Bill Stockwell thanked committee chairpersons by using color slides of their faces on bodies depicting their role in the Association. The sketches by Sue Stecker were accompanied by humorous verses composed by "Rosedale Ruth" Stockwell. For Bill Mathers, head of the summer recreation program, the verse was: Of baseBALL you have often heard; But BaseBILL is the newer word. It MATHERS not what time of day – He's ready – ANYTIME – to play!

The verse for George Harding, *Tattler* editor, was: "He fills his day with honest toil, and then he burns the midnight oil, He edits things with vim and zest – He Tattles last who Tattles best." Of Brad Smith and Jim McLernon, Winter Recreation, it was said: "When winds do howl and snowflakes fly, You might meet up with either guy, By the skating rink, You'll find them there, Attired in thermal underwear."

The problem of distributing the

Caricatures of Association committee chairmen

Tattler was an ongoing problem for the organization for many years, often resulting in residents getting short notice of the group's monthly meeting. After much discussion, the local Cub Scout troop agreed to deliver the *Tattler* to Park residents and was paid $50 a month in 1965. Two years later, a new distribution method was employed.

The *Rosedale Tattler* got a new editor in August 1967, as Burt Stoddard took over from George Harding, who had served for 15½ years. As the times changed and more and more women were employed outside the home, women's first names were used in some issues. Yet, in those same issues, the traditional reference, as in Mrs. Robert Campbell, was still employed.

The Community House Expands

In February 1961, the board made plans for a $9000, two-story addition to the Community House on the east end to provide for a backstage area, additional storage, second-floor meeting room, restrooms and drinking fountain. Woman's Club president Belva Lacey presented $1000 to the Association for the addition. Park Players made a $2000 donation. Even the children joined in. The children from Shaftsbury won $5 for their June Day float and donated the money to the Association's building fund.

Leaders break ground for Community House addition, 1961
l-r: Allan Stecker, building operations, Association President Robert Rutherford, Woman's Club President Louise Reading and Lyle Reading, building chairman

Officers and members of the Association and Woman's Club gathered for a groundbreaking ceremony June 21, and construction was completed by early September. Morris Webster (Greenview), an architect and engineer and designer of the original Community House, designed the addition. Wilbur Lockwood (Huntington) of Lockwood-McCutcheon Co. served as the general contractor.

Other improvements followed: a new marquee on the front of the Community House in 1964, along with a canopy and vestibule, for $2910; installation of new sinks and counters in the kitchen; new sheet metal roof on the skating shelter and equipment garage in 1967; and landscaping with the assistance of the Boy and Girl Scouts and area garden clubs. Funds were set aside to install new lighting around the Community House.

Taking advantage of technology, the NRPCA installed a phone in the Community House office and later answering equipment in September 1963. Residents were encouraged to call 837-3416 for information and to make reservations for the facility. Nearly 60 years later, the number is still the same!

New marquee at the Community House

Begging Makes Its Return

In the early days of North Rosedale Park, begging (trick-or-treating) was an acceptable practice. Then things got out of hand, with children being brought to Rosedale Park; derogatory comments made about treats; and children still begging at 10 and 11 p.m. In response, the Woman's Club created three separate Halloween parties to entertain the children and teens in the neighborhood. That practice worked well for years but gradually children began to clamor to go trick-or-treating.

The issue came to a head in 1961-62. For the first time in about 12 years, the Woman's Club decided not to sponsor Halloween activities for children in response to a petition signed by 262 parents favoring trick-or-treating in the Park, in addition to the dance for teenagers. Since several other areas in the city permitted begging and sponsored activities for youth, the Woman's Club honored the request but indicated it could not assume the responsibility of supervising begging for such a large area. The Club did agree with two of the suggestions and added two of its own: Beggars should be under parental supervision and begging should be limited to children too young to attend the dance for teenagers. So begging returned to the delight of the children of North Rosedale Park.

Woman's Club and Civic Association Work in Tandem

Rosedale Park Woman's Club turned 40 and celebrated the occasion with an elegant anniversary ball in March 1964. As part of the celebration, *That Wonderful Year*, a play depicting the early days of the Woman's Club, was presented with insight provided by Rebecca Rutherford. As a youngster, she saw first-hand the development of North Rosedale Park as her father, Charles Erickson, served as the Shelden company's sales manager and handled all property.

A special membership drive was launched with the Civic Association in 1965 to encourage residents to join their organizations. Association dues were $10, and Woman's Club dues were $7 with a $2 initiation fee. By September 1966, the membership drive was deemed a success – 1000 members for the Association, 600 plus for the Woman's Club – enabling the Club to retain its distinction as the largest of its kind in the metro Detroit area.

One success followed another. The Ramblin' Round Rosedale event, sponsored by the Woman's Club in October 1965, featured a tour of seven homes – the precursor to the Home & Garden Tour. A highlight was the home at 16739 Shaftsbury designed by Lancelot Sukert, architect of the Scarab Club in the Cultural Center. The home featured beams in Swedish primitive design, a hand-painted mural, Pewabic tile trim in the powder room, and a painting by famed muralist Diego Rivera. Tea and shopping followed at the Community House, with the event raising $1619 to support eyeglasses, braces, crutches, and dentures for seniors.

Ramblin' Round Rosedale Tour, 16739 Shaftsbury

Equally important were the activities sponsored by the Junior Activities Committee of the Woman's Club. Local deejays were employed to spin the records at the teen dances. One such DJ in October 1965 was none other than Dick Purtan of WKNR, a popular radio station in the '50s and '60s. The Woman's Club landed "The Buoys," a popular rock band in the Detroit area, for the junior high dance a few years later.

Christmas breakfast at the Community House drew 700 residents later that year to see the beautiful decorations representing "The 12 Days of Christmas," created by the Woman's Club. The next year, 800 attended as more than $400 was generated for the Association.

"What a wonderful year this has been! We have learned so much at the do-it-yourself sessions, been exposed to culture and the arts, and have been delightfully entertained at the social gatherings. Thanks to the efficient planning of the program committee, they have left us with many lovely memories to cherish and have taught us many new projects we will do in the future for our own personal pleasure." Marjorie Koepke, Woman's Club Vice President in the organization's 1966 annual report.

In spite of these successes, women's membership in the NRPCA remained elusive. Maybe it was a subtle hint about opening the Association to women, but Winnifred Dunn wrote to the president in July 1964. "We enclose our check for $10 to cover annual dues. We realize that women are not eligible for membership but nevertheless we are pleased to contribute as we too benefit from the good work of your group in maintaining high standards for the Park." Dunn's support of the Association represented a growing interest of the women in joining the Civic Association.

Finally, in September 1964, a committee was established to consider changes to the by-laws to accommodate women in some capacity. President Wigle appointed Walter Bieneman, Holland Weir, Herbert Schoenberg, D.E. Batey and William Wickham to the committee. After the study and a lengthy report, the committee recommended in October that the Association "not amend its by-laws, but leave this matter exactly as it now exists." The committee's recommendation was approved, and the inclusion of women in the Association was not to be – that day.

There It is ... Again!

Vandalism was rampant around the Community House during the summer of 1966, "far exceeding such attacks in any previous period." The list: exterior doors left open, water running in the restroom, damage to interior and exterior doors, holes gouged in garage roof, broken windows, fire started in the skating shelter, hinges broken off garage door and articles stolen. Rather than wag their collective fingers, Association leaders vowed to turn all matters over to the Detroit Police Department for action.

While teens may have been out of control elsewhere, they knew how to behave when they visited Ed's Sweet Shop, owned by Mr. and Mrs. Ed Panzner since 1930. "We are very proud of our record and can recall only five youths (of the hundreds who have bought penny candy or ice cream cones) who didn't turn out to be good men or women," said Mrs. Ed. "Some people think we've been a little strict with the boys and girls, but ... we've always been able to straighten out the various problems ourselves."

In an effort to address vandalism and increase safety, Association members investigated utilizing a private patrol service for the neighborhood. Pat Ward, who had provided protection services in the Park for the past 20 years, proposed adding a marked patrol car with a telephone and operating the service as a private contractor on a fee basis, covered by Park residents.

A total of 586 residents of the 600 needed eventually signed up for the service, scheduled to begin September 1. For $3 a month, residents could connect directly with patrolmen from 8 p.m. - 5 a.m. to report suspicious activity, plus arrange for a patrolman to check their homes while on vacation or out for the evening.

Before the service really got started, there was talk of it ending in December 1967. Why? Residents had failed to follow through on their commitment. In such a short time, NRPCA President Dave McCabe said the results of the increased patrols were evident. "Disturbances around the Community House have been broken up as have several drinking parties. The number of cars parking on the side streets have been reduced, and who knows how much budding trouble didn't happen because the patrol car appeared in the vicinity at the right time?"

Over and over, Association leaders pleaded with residents to pay their bills so the Ward Patrol wouldn't be forced to cut service. Former and current Park residents recognize this song and dance.

Finally, Association members and residents decided it was time to get tough to curtail the vandalism and incidents of foul language, drinking and likely drug use at the Community House. The Police Department, represented by Lt. Miller from the 16th Precinct, agreed to increase area patrols and make arrests whenever necessary. Signs were posted to indicate park closures; and plans were completed to install new lighting and other security measures. "The incidents MUST and WILL be stopped," said NRPCA President August Blomquist. "Let's not let a few ruin our community for all." Residents were encouraged to submit ideas for programs and activities in order to make North Rosedale "a more interesting and satisfying place for the restless, but generally fine group of teenagers who reside here."

Park Players Continue Stellar Performances

The women took the stage in November 1963 for *The Women*, which included 29 women and two brave men. The play, written by Clare Boothe Luce, focused on the lives and power struggles of a group of women and the gossip that propels and damages their relationships.

Park Players staged one of America's favorite plays, *Gentlemen Prefer Blondes*, in April 1966. Director Frank Jakes challenged the cast before its first performance. "There are two types of shows: 'professional amateur' and 'amateur amateur,' and it's up to the cast to determine which this show will be." The show was seen by more than 1,300 patrons over five performances, and the general response was the show was the former, a big hit.

Former President Bill Stockwell said this in 1969: "This writer has seen most of the Park Players shows since those early days when it all started with the men's minstrel shows and he has handled lights and curtains and staging for several of them and has even appeared in

Verna Finly starred in the Park Players' production of *Gentlemen Prefer Blondes*

a few without making any appreciable dent in theatrical history. It's his opinion that the *My Fair Lady* staged by Park Players in April is clearly among the two or three finest the group has ever produced."

After attending *Pajama Game* by Park Players at the Association's Ladies Night in May 1961, Judd Arnett, a columnist for the *Detroit Free Press* and Grandmont resident, noted, "Let it be remembered that someone once described Detroit as 'a series of small towns hung together by the sinews of streets and highways,' and the other night the truth of this was brought closer to home. I have lived long enough (darn it) to learn one thing: that there is no worthwhile substitute for community life, for gathering with friends in behalf of projects or causes, or just in the spirit of fun. A big city can be the loneliest place on Earth if you are out of things … That doesn't happen in North Rosedale Park: those extroverts out there have plenty of 'togetherness!' "

Park residents came together for the annual park cleanup day in 1961. Although the turnout was light, the Park children were there to help. "Thank Heaven we have children," said Karl Klapka, the Association's grounds chairman. The kids merely had to show their blisters from raking to receive free pop.

The Association at Work for Residents

The Association prided itself on keeping residents informed on a variety of topics, including construction of the Jeffries, Chrysler and Fisher freeways, baseball diamond improvements and the loss of trees due to Dutch Elm disease.

Just in time for the 1967 baseball season, improvements were made to the baseball diamond including a new backstop and protective fencing at a cost of $1000. The improvements were made possible through donations to the Richard Mathers Memorial Fund, set up to honor the teen who was hit and killed in July 1966. New benches also were installed.

The Dutch Elm Disease was still wreaking havoc across the city and in the Park. According to the City's Forestry Department, the North Rosedale area had lost almost 400 trees during 1964-66.

"There was a time in Rosedale when there were humongous trees. The streets were lined with these wonderful trees. They were so beautiful," said Nancy Kelel, who lived on Gainsborough. "Then those trees died. It was just devastating and that was a major loss."

To encourage tree planting, the Association agreed to pay up to $12.50 to members who replaced a tree.

Association members approved constitution revisions to add a membership secretary; revise the process for non-resident members; and increase yearly membership dues from $10 to $12. The cost of a Civic Association membership inched up slightly to $15 by 1970.

Although the United States had entered the Vietnam War, the war was rarely mentioned in the *Tattler*. One reference, a letter from Captain David Dearing to his sister, contained a very simple request. "You asked what you could do for me, and the answer is a simple plea for a simple commodity – soap. The area is so infested with the Viet Cong that normal supplies are difficult to receive. So dear sister, I certainly would appreciate anything you can do; even scraps of soap would be usable. I know that the people down in that little district would be very grateful." Dee Hayward, 16524 Shaftsbury, got to work gathering bars of soap from neighbors and shipped several shoe boxes of soap to her brother in 1966.

The war, however, was the focus of the Association's monthly meeting in September 1966. "Why Vietnam?" was the meeting theme as two films were shown courtesy of the Naval and Marine Corps Reserve training center of Detroit. The Association also began mailing copies of the *Tattler* to residents serving during the Vietnam War.

North Rosedale lost one of its oldest and most enthusiastic residents with the death of Virgil Zetterlind in January 1967. Zett was a co-founder of the Detroit Amateur Baseball Federation and supported sandlot baseball for 53 years. He also served as the North Rosedale Park bowling league secretary for 22 years and bowling editor for the *Tattler*.

There's a First Time for Everything

Speaking about her work ministering to the poor, Rev. Charleszetta "Mother" Waddles became the first African American to speak to NRPCA members at their monthly meeting in April 1968. Waddles talked about future plans to expand services at the Perpetual Mission Soup Kitchen. "Through the mission and kitchen, I shock people into realizing they're good then they start thinking about how they used to go to church. That's the only way to help these people."

In the June 1968 *Tattler*, the editor pointed out the level of education that students received at Cooke School and Redford High School. "The quality of education offered North Rosedale students by the public schools serving our community has been – and remains – high." His proof: Based on Iowa test scores, eighth-graders at Cooke averaged at or near the ninth grade level in achievement from 1964-1967. The actual figures ranged from 8.8 to 9. Based on both ability and achievement tests, Redford high school students ranked next to the highest of Detroit's comprehensive high schools. In science, Redford students ranked first.

As school approached in the fall of 1968, there were concerns, once again, regarding the possibility that students from outside the area could be bused in to attend Cooke School. Based on conversations with several high-ranking Detroit school officials, the *Tattler* editor said the rumors were false. One school official

Cooke School

said, "We wouldn't want to hurt a good learning situation at the school by deliberately forcing class sizes higher." That news probably relieved North Rosedale parents, at least for the moment.

Girl Scouts celebrate founder Juliette Low's birthday at the Community House, March 1960 l-r: Cathy Guth, Kathy Rand, Diane Weiss, Karen Young, Maureen Merkel, Cherry Cyrol, Sally Wickham, Janet Graybill, Gloria Lukasik, Margery Martin, Lois Rutt and Donna Sturwold.

Park children participate in 4th of July talent show, July 1960

THE 1970S

The turbulence of the 1960s gave way in the 1970s to calls for an end to segregation, redlining and blockbusting, and movement toward integration in public schools, housing and neighborhoods. In North Rosedale Park, those issues were front and center as the neighborhood went through a painful transition as African-American families integrated the all-white neighborhood. Even as tensions at times ran high, North Rosedale Park organizations celebrated milestones and continued efforts to make the Park better for residents.

Detroit Mayor Roman Gribbs and family, 1970
l-r: Paula, Katherine, Christopher, Rebecca and Carla

The decade began with Roman S. Gribbs, 16515 Edinborough, being sworn in as mayor of Detroit in January. Rather than moving to the Manoogian Mansion, the official mayoral residence, Mayor Gribbs and his family remained in the Park during his tenure. Working with the Mayor were Park residents Mary Ball, 15892 Rosemont, executive secretary of the Mayor's committee for the Cultural Center and director of the City's International Visitors Program; and Jacob Sobieraj, 18565 Bretton Drive, president of the Detroit Department of Parks and Recreation Commission. Daniel Krichbaum, 15717 Rosemont, later served as the director of the Parks and Recreation Department under Mayor Coleman Young, and Lyle Reading, 18535 Lancashire, was chief sanitary engineer with the Buildings and Safety Engineering Department.

The Evolution of NRPCA

Like many organizations of that era, the Association was slow to admit women as members. When the idea of female members arose in 1964, the proposal was voted down. Past President August Blomquist proposed that the Association sample the membership to determine if women should be accepted as members. After a prolonged debate, 24 voted to conduct the survey while 23 opposed.

With women in mind, the Association sponsored a panel discussion in November 1970 on the women's liberation movement, expecting to draw a crowd and generate some controversy. The meeting featured representatives from several women's action groups and was moderated by Barbara Hitsky, "Women in Today's World" columnist at *The Detroit News*.

A seismic shift took place the next year, as the Association sought to finally extend membership to female property owners and widows. Five amendments were considered at the December 1971 meeting: 1) allow widows and other female heads of households as members; 2) allow residents of Greenview, Avon and Stahelin between McNichols and Puritan to become members; 3) accept business owners operating within the boundaries of North Rosedale Park as non-voting members; 4) permit Association meetings to occur on nights other than the second Friday; and 5) expand the board from 9 to 12 members.

The proposals to expand the board and to provide flexibility in scheduling meetings were approved in January 1972. Three months later, in April, the membership agreed to allow women to become members and to allow Stahelin, Greenview and Avon residents and North Rosedale Park business owners to become members and serve on committees but not vote or hold office.

For the first time, women were elected to the NRPCA board in January 1973: Christine Armstrong, membership secretary; Betty Grigg, recording secretary; and Irene Matheson and Winifred Sawyer, directors. Pleased with the results, Charles Allegrina, outgoing NRPCA President, noted: "Their participation is going to bring about some changes and it will all be to the good."

Later changes allowed Greenview, Stahelin and Avon homeowners to become voting (active) members; revised directors' terms so that they were staggered; and made membership secretary, recording secretary and treasurer appointed rather than elected positions.

In May 1974, the board approved the creation of a reservation secretary to handle reservations for the Community House, obtain board

NRPCA Board includes women for first time, 1973

approvals, collect all monies and coordinate use of the facility. Later amendments included making the wives and widows of life members eligible for life memberships and making the widows of active members who resided and owned property in the Park and lived in the neighborhood for 30 years eligible to become life members.

Don Ball, *Detroit News* reporter

Among the Association's many prominent speakers in the '70s was Don Ball, 15892 Rosemont. Ball shared his groundbreaking work for *The Detroit News* that exposed corruption and mismanagement in the U.S. Department of Housing and Urban Development (HUD). Ball's writing on the subject in late 1970 led to an investigation by U.S. Attorney Ralph Guy, resulting in more than 100 persons convicted and others indicted and awaiting trial. His work earned him numerous awards including United Press International's 1971 award for best general reporting in Michigan.

Other high-profile speakers included Mayor Coleman Young in March 1976, Police Commander Jacob Martin (16th Precinct) in April and newly appointed Police Chief William Hart in November. Mayor Young's appearance in 1976 drew an overflow crowd. He was back to speak in November 1978.

Rosedale Tattler Gets a New Look

Following a contest to redesign the masthead, the winning design by Norma Zemke was unveiled in September 1970. Zemke said, "I've always liked and appreciated art, but didn't claim any real talent. When I saw your contest announced, I thought, 'what the heck, I could

Rosedale Park Tattler gets new masthead, 1970

try.' " And try she did – and won. Zemke lived at 15837 Avon with her husband, Dave, and two daughters. Her full name was listed with the new masthead story, consistent with the emerging trends in the *Tattler*.

Another progressive move was naming Adelaide Stoddard as editor of the *Rosedale Tattler* in March 1971, a position normally held by a male member. However, husband Burt Stoddard remained on as an advisor. Adelaide was a former writer, editor and public relations director.

In recognition of the Association's 50th Anniversary in 1974, the masthead included a rose. Four years later, the *Tattler* got a new editor, Sally Evalt, who replaced Betty Grigg. Evalt had a journalism background and served as the editor of Kmart's national newspaper.

Community House Improvements

With support from American Legion Post 390, which met in the building, the NRPCA added air conditioning in 1970, and more improvements in 1973 – paneled walls, acoustical ceiling, special lighting and new red carpeting. Planned or completed improvements in 1978 included parking lot repaving, outdoor water fountain replacement, thermal insulating windows on the south wall, and security lights on the corners of the building. A $15,000 renovation the next year included constructing wooden columns and updated electrical in the auditorium, and new draperies in the auditorium, balcony and lobby. Don Schieble, Park resident and registered architect, was the project manager. Members approved borrowing $10,000 for the project at the April 1979 meeting.

Following City Council action to institute a 10 p.m. to 6 a.m. curfew for privately-owned parks, as requested by the NRPCA, a curfew was put into effect on the Community House grounds in 1970. Helping to enforce the curfew was Pat Ward, owner of the private patrol company. In recognition of his 25 years of keeping Park residents safe, April 9, 1971 was designated Pat Ward Night. Ward shared stories ranging from scaring burglars to chasing speeders to checking homes for vacationing residents. Four months later, he passed away. His son, John, continued the patrol service.

Trying to Get Control of the Youth

The proliferation of drugs in the 1960s simply carried over into the 1970s, and North Rosedale Park could not escape the harsh reality. The NRPCA worked tirelessly to address the problem, including bringing in speakers. Dr. Aaron Rutledge, a recognized expert, spoke on "The Family in the Midst of the Drug Culture" in December 1971.

Yet, it wasn't always the Association doing all the work. Several teen residents suggested creating a junior NRPCA and providing alternate activities for teens just wanting to hang out in the Park. The board accepted the idea, and Dr. Paul Fitzpatrick and Katherine Gribbs served as the group's advisors. The first officers were Jim Stella, president; Paul McNamara, vice president; Chuck Esser, treasurer; and Greg Uhl, programs and entertainment. The new group started Truck Stop, a coffee house for teens, in 1971. Proceeds from the coffee house were sent to organizations fighting drug abuse.

Truck Stop flyer, December 1971

Some of the group's leaders were heading to college in 1972 and were seeking others to keep the coffee house going. "The Truck Stop is an important part of the community and just because people are going to college, there is no sense of stopping it now. So I urge all of you to try to help your community and to join the Truck Stop," said Paul McNamara.

While programs were part of the solution, the Association and residents were determined to address the most obvious problem: flourishing drug activity right on the Community House grounds. After a two-month surveillance operation in July 1971, the Detroit police arrested 34 young people at the park and their homes for the illegal sale and possession of drugs. Confiscated were three pounds of marijuana, one pound of hashish, 1,000 doses of LSD and a small quantity of heroin, most of which was taken from the homes of those arrested.

"Arresting young people isn't going to wipe out Detroit's drug problem," said Lt. Howard Austin, Detroit Police Narcotics Unit coordinator. "But it may have enough impact on some to stop them from doing it again, and it reduces the chances that other youngsters will be enticed down the same path."

Fighting Against Solicitation and Blockbusting

During the 1970s, the residents and leaders of North Rosedale Park were dealing with challenges on so many fronts – drugs, white flight, integration of the neighborhood and schools, unscrupulous real estate companies and busing.

A 1962 City ordinance put stricter controls on methods used to promote house sales as a means of reducing so-called blockbusting – the practice of persuading owners to sell property cheaply based on fear that people of another race or class were moving into the neighborhood, and then profiting by reselling at a higher price. The ordinance, supported by the NRPCA, set the location and number of for sale signs on property; forbid signs on property not for sale and City-owned property; and forbid signs indicating a property had been sold. It also made it unlawful to list race in real estate advertising or listings.

Even with the ordinance in place, it didn't stop real estate companies or individuals from trying to skirt the law or steering individuals away from certain neighborhoods and cities. When that didn't work, real estate agents and neighborhood organizations worked together to develop point systems and committees to screen and approve potential home-buyers. Park resident Mary Davis remembers that period as a young adult. "It was really ugly. I would answer the phone, and I would immediately get hit with 'Are you considering selling your home? You better get out now or you won't get anything for your home.' "

In 1972, the North Rosedale Park, Emerson and Rosedale Park neighborhoods took the ultimate step to stop the practice: a lawsuit. In Zuch v. Hussey, a racially-mixed group brought suit against a group of 12 real estate companies and agents charged with either steering on a racial basis or soliciting real estate listings. Attorneys John F. Burns and Ted Rosenberg, both Shaftsbury residents, handled the case for the homeowners without charge. Plaintiffs requested a court order for a preliminary injunction to stop both the steering and solicitation.

Because of additional costs with the case, NRPCA past President Charles Allegrina was forced to remind residents of how their support helped in the fight against blockbusting. "Each civic association bears one third of the expense and the money comes from dues – your dues – no where else," he said.

It would take three years, but finally a preliminary hearing was held in 1975 before Judge Damon J. Keith, Eastern District of Michigan/Southern Division, and lasted 10 weeks.

Zuch v. Hussey, 1972

The three associations scored a big victory on March 14, 1975, when Judge Keith found that there was proof of blockbusting and steering by the defendants and granted the plaintiff's motion for a preliminary injunction. His ruling prohibited 12 real estate firms from telephone, mail or personal solicitation of property sales listings unless first contacted by a homeowner. It underlined the prohibition against directing buyers to certain areas because of their race. The court order was a preliminary injunction, which is still in effect. The case has never been tried.

Burns reminded residents that the fight against blockbusting was not over. "It is more important than ever that the kinds of solicitation barred by the court order be reported by all residents immediately. The court has indicated it will deal firmly with any violations, but it must know about them first."

One defendant, Bowers Realty & Investment Company, appealed, and the decision was reversed for that defendant as to solicitation only. The decision was otherwise upheld. Burns and Rosenberg were honored by the three associations at a party in April 1975. Vince Zuch and his wife Rita, the plaintiffs in the case, were honored for their work in organizing and coordinating the out-of-court activities for the lawsuit.

People Moving Out, People Moving In

In response to a variety of challenges facing the community, a group of concerned residents formed the North Rosedale Park Forum in 1971 to study and address contemporary social problems, including developing greater understanding among ethnic groups.

As attitudes toward minorities slowly changed and whites left the city, individuals looking to improve their quality of life were drawn to neighborhoods like North Rosedale Park. As Black families moved to the Park in the early 1970s, their experiences with residents were mixed. The response of some residents was to move as quickly as possible. Of those who stayed, most were accepting or at least kept their feelings to themselves. Yet there were some who didn't exactly roll out the welcome mat.

Fred Russell Sr., an African American, moved with his family to Lancashire in August 1974. His son, Fred (Ricky) Russell Jr., was nine at the time. Russell (Ricky) said his experience living in North Rosedale was very pleasant overall, but he did recall a number of occasions when he faced racism. "Things were thrown at me," Russell said. "I was chased a couple of times. Once I jumped our fence after being chased and the kids were right behind, but when they saw my neighbor they ran away." He was thankful for his neighbor's intervention.

One experience really hurt and was hard to forget. "I remember I was in a fight one time. An adult pulled up and I explained what happened and that it wasn't my fault. His response:

'That's why we don't want you over here.' "

Tess Tchou had a totally different experience with racism. When she and her husband, Ray, moved to the Park in August 1977, "The lady who lived north of us couldn't wait to tell us that she was glad that we moved there," said Tchou, who is Filipino. "She was living alone and based on some of the things that she said, it let me know that she was fearful (of minorities moving into the neighborhood)."

For Susan Miller Erickson, racism wasn't something that she saw exhibited or embraced. "There was color and there really wasn't color for us. We played sports together and went to parties together," she said. "It was a changing time in the neighborhood. We were kids and we don't see this racism, not like all the adults."

During the years prior to Blacks moving to North Rosedale, there was another type of discrimination at work: classism. "It was very much of a WASP neighborhood," said Mary Ellen McEvoy, a former Park resident. (WASP refers to White Anglo-Saxon Protestants, a social group of white Protestants, who are typically wealthy and well-connected.[1]) "It was a totally segregated neighborhood. If you were Black, Hispanic, Italian, Jewish, you weren't able to move here." As she was considering moving to North Rosedale, "My dad said, 'You get your kids into the neighborhood because they are going to integrate. That's how you want your kids to grow up.' "

As Blacks moved in, whites moved out along with their attitudes. "For my husband and I, it was fine that they left. For us, it was a welcome change from the uppity attitude," said McEvoy. "Rosedale had a snobbish tier to it. There was that white, haughty attitude; not just white, but being of a certain status."

Depending on who you talked to, the factors that contributed to white flight vary: the 1967 riots; construction of the freeways; 1970s recession; Blacks moving to white neighborhoods; and busing. Some even pointed to the election of Coleman Young in 1973 as Detroit's first Black mayor as a factor. Hard-charging, outspoken and unapologetic, Mayor Young quickly polarized Detroiters into two camps: love him or hate him. Most Black Detroiters consider Young a legend and liberator; many whites believe he was a corrupt militant who disliked white people.[2]

Tom Ridgway, who grew up in North Rosedale and still resides in the Park, said when Mayor Young was elected a lot of people sold their homes. "I feel bad that many people call him a racist and a crook," said Ridgway. "I hear all of these comments about him, but they really don't know him." Ridgway, who is Caucasian, had a distinct vantage point; his mother, June Ridgway Roselle, served under Mayor Young as head of the Assessors Office and then the Civic Center Department.

Ridgway recalled one incident that bothered him. Mayor Young knew his family and was a pallbearer at his father's funeral. "Our friends were saying 'why is he here?' Being around white people, they think they can say anything or make offensive remarks," Ridgway added.

School Busing: The Final Straw

For many white families still residing in Detroit, the implementation of busing in 1976 was the proverbial nail in the coffin. There was talk of desegregation all across the country, but Detroit took center stage in the Bradley v. Milliken case. On August 18, 1970, the NAACP filed suit against Michigan state officials, including Governor William Milliken. The NAACP argued that although schools were not officially segregated, the City of Detroit and the State of Michigan had enacted policies to increase racial segregation in schools and should be obligated to desegregate them. The NAACP also suggested there was a direct relationship between unfair housing practices and educational segregation.

The lawsuit was affirmed by Judge Stephen Roth, U.S. District Court, in 1971 who ordered cross-district busing between predominantly Black Detroit and its predominantly white suburbs. In response

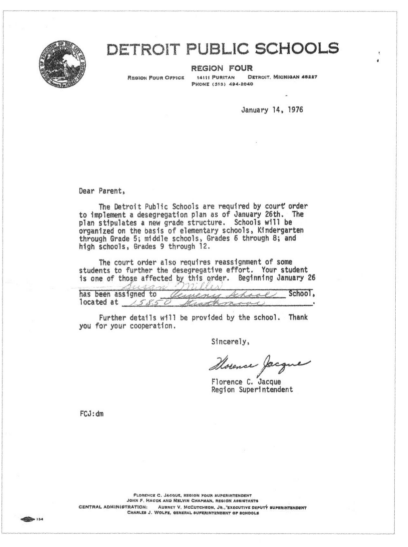

Susan Miller's letter regarding busing to Cerveny, 1976

to his ruling, NRPCA president Lawrence O'Connor argued strongly before the Central Board of Education in opposition to the busing plan and in support of a voluntary plan and neighborhood schools. In his opinion, only a tiny minority of the 1400 families in North Rosedale Park were "outright racist and bigots." The vast majority "hold varying degrees of social consciousness, and social conscience, who, though affluent, higher-than-average taxpayers, feel an obligation to help the disadvantaged in matters of safety, education, opportunity.

"We are tired of, and we resent, the expectation on the part of a segment of the community, that we should feel guilty about our affluence. One of the rewards for getting ahead in the world is buying a better house in a better neighborhood where the schools reflect an educational attitude representative of that type of neighborhood ... We feel any effort to deny our children the fruits of our labor by sending them to schools in the inner city is definitely directly opposed to the American way."

In its ruling on the matter in 1972, the U.S. Circuit Court affirmed Judge Roth's ruling. In July 1974, however, the United States Supreme Court overturned the plan and ordered that a Detroit-only busing plan be put into place. Assigned to the case, U.S. District Judge Robert DeMascio approved a busing plan in 1976, where about 30,000 students were reassigned. Another 30,000 changed schools to comply with the order that reorganized the grade structure in Detroit schools. Kindergarten through fifth grades were elementary. Sixth through eighth grades were in middle or junior high schools. High schools had ninth-12th grades.

Julianne Lyons, then an eighth-grader at Cooke School, was part of the first class of kids bused to Cerveny Middle School in January 1976 and hated it. "I wanted to graduate from the school where my dad attended and all of my cousins went there too." She was bused in the middle of her last year at Cooke School.

The talk of busing drove many North Rosedale families out of public schools and out of the city during the years prior to 1976. "People were moving out and running for the suburbs. Or they were scrambling to get their kids in Catholic schools – St. Scholastica and Christ the King," said Lyons, who lives in her family home on Glastonbury.

For Daniel Bellware, busing also was a low point. "A lot of us lost track of each other after that happened," said Bellware, who was bused from Cooke to Cerveny. "Everyone scattered and several, like my family, moved away. The neighborhood lost one of its anchors when Cooke School ceased to be a neighborhood school."

Going to a new school was difficult for white students from Cooke, especially as the Black students at Cerveny retaliated. "We had rocks thrown at us because we were in their neighborhood. They didn't want us there. It was awful, throwing rocks, spitting at us and pulling up girls' skirts," said Susan Miller Erickson, who grew up on Lancashire. "It destroyed the sense of community with the K-8 students in Rosedale Park. It was supposed to be better for everyone. But I think our neighborhood suffered."

While there were situations during the 1970s that did not make Park residents proud, many current and former residents point to life in the Park as being good, almost idyllic. From sunup to sundown, the streets, playground and islands (to the chagrin of Association leaders) were filled with kids everywhere, running, playing and having a great time.

"There were kids everywhere, and coming in and out of each other's houses. It was an absolute sense of belonging and community," said Nancy Kelel, who lived on Gainsborough and still visits regularly. "You knew everybody and everybody knew you. When you see the world and neighborhoods today, we know how good we had it. It was such a magical place."

Lyons describes a similar experience. "Every house had at least three kids. There were some pretty big Catholic families here in the neighborhood. Then we would play hide-n-seek over a three-block area, running through people's backyards, on roofs ... We would play a game of 500 (like baseball) in the middle of the street. We were everywhere."

Despite some bad experiences, Fred Russell Jr. (Ricky) is quick to say that he enjoyed growing up in the Park. "You walked to school and we knew who lived where. In the summer, we would go door to door to get enough people to play whatever we were going to play that day. It was a nice neighborhood. I experienced way more of that. You knew who your neighbors were and that creates security."

Boy Scouts at June Day 1977

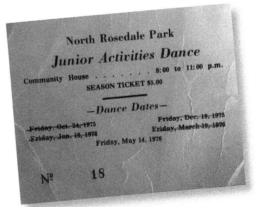

JA Dance Ticket 1976

Association Works On Behalf of Residents

The aroma of barbecue filled the air as the Association held its Steak Roast in 1972, marking five years of the annual event held every September. The cookout, which began in 1967, had different names – Fall Barbecue and Corn Roast, Western Chuck Wagon and Steak Out – but Steak Roast was the name that finally stuck.

The Association established the Environmental Planning Group in 1973, a new organization headed by Bill Butler, to protect and improve the Park's physical appearance – boulevards, entrances, Cooke School area, traffic control, Grandland, business strips, expressway and landscaping.

Like the rest of the city, North Rosedale Park was still dealing with the Dutch Elm Disease. The Association authorized $100 to cover experimental treatment of trees at the Community House that had been tagged for removal. The NRPCA's efforts to inform residents of ways to prevent the spread of the disease were recognized by the Michigan Department of Highways and Transportation (Keep Michigan Beautiful Inc.) as it presented North Rosedale with a distinguished service award in October 1975.

No matter the decade, it was always a challenge to convince residents to join the Association or pay for the private patrol service or snow removal. John Ward expressed his concern to the board about not obtaining enough new members to maintain the private patrol service. Snow removal was equally a problem. Everyone wanted it, yet not everyone was willing to pay.

North Rosedale Park Civic Association

December 1973
420 members

February 1975
559 members

April 1976
579 members

April 1978
786 members

February 1979
717 members

September 1979
940 members

Among the various complaints from Park residents, parking on narrow streets and dogs were probably near the top. "It's about dogs. I've lived here for years and never seen so many dogs running loose. There are three dogs or more on my block alone whose owners love them so much they like the dogs to be 'free' ... What's 'freedom' when we can't keep our yards nice or even walk outside without being threatened?" Ashton resident

In an effort to bring City services closer to residents, the Police Department opened a new mini police station at 15916 Puritan between Southfield and Greenfield. In 1975, the Northwest Neighborhood City Hall opened at 20344 West McNichols at Stout, bringing services to the neighborhoods, such as dog and bicycle licenses; voter registration; senior citizen bus cards; and speakers for community meetings. The office got a new name and new location in 1979 when the Far West Neighborhood City Hall relocated to 19426 Grand River in North Rosedale Park.

Celebrating Milestones

In celebration of its 50th anniversary, the Woman's Club held a Friendship Luncheon in October 1973 and showed two films that chronicled the early days and the neighborhood in the 1940s and 1950s. The event included a fashion show highlighting trends from 1923 to 1970.

The Association followed with its own celebration, marking its 50th anniversary with a birthday party that drew 265 people and included a skit reflecting the decades. The event culminated

Former presidents and board members of Park Players, 1978
l-r: Howard Meade, John Burns, Winnie Sawyer, Mike VanDeKeere, Bill Renner, Carol Stinson, Stan Taylor, Sharon Lippe, Roger Holt, Barb Davidson, Tom Sawyer and Dennis Davidson

with the Gold Ball, a dinner dance on October 26. "Be a party crasher ... The cat's pajamas. Be a swell. Groove it, baby, at the Gold Ball for the NRPCA at the Community House October 26. Bring your sugar pie and dance to the music of 'The Good Times Band' and eat dinner from Al Sayres for a fantastic price of $20 per couple." Teaser in October 1974 *Tattler*

The celebration provided an opportunity to recognize some of the Park's oldest residents and pioneers – names like Arthur, Browne, Bryan, Corsette, Eddy, Grier, Harley, Holden, Judson, Lannin, Lillie, Porath, Siebert, Sloman, Spencer, Squiers, Summerlee, Wehmeyer and Wilcox. Included were three residents who moved to the Park as children – Clarke Archbold (his father, Harry, was a *Tattler* editor and Rosedale Park directory publisher), Alban Norris Jr. (his father, Alban Sr., was a *Tattler* editor and Association photographer) and Lyle Reading, the Rosedale Park historian.

Park Players followed suit and honored its past presidents with the dedication of a plaque for display at the Community House in June 1975.

The Association also established a new legal fund to cover costs that had previously come out of the general fund. The fund allowed residents and other interested parties to contribute directly to cover legal matters, such as the case of the realtor suit. To benefit the legal fund, the Association booked Josh White Jr., a popular folk singer. White was such a draw and a crowd favorite that he appeared in concert in North Rosedale another five times in the 1970s.

"I thoroughly enjoyed myself at your community house, everyone was very responsive to my style of singing. I'm flattered to be invited back and I'm looking forward to it. It's like coming home to old friends." North Rosedale must have grown on White too, as he eventually purchased a home in the Park. "It's even a bigger thrill because this is home," White said. "It's the only gig I've ever had where I can walk to work."

In 1976, the nation celebrated the Bicentennial – the 200th birthday of the United States – and North Rosedale Park joined the party. The Woman's Club created a Bicentennial cookbook and memorial tablecloth and sponsored a box supper and square dance. The American Legion Post 390 hosted a Bi-

Josh White flyer – June Day 1978

centennial cookout. The Association invited Judge Roman Gribbs as the guest of honor for its June 10 dinner meeting, followed by June Day with a Bicentennial theme. Park Players produced *Oklahoma*. Cooke School combined its 50th anniversary and the Bicentennial into one big party, which included presentations and student performances. Detroit Public Schools Superintendent Dr. Arthur Jefferson also attended the June event.

A major strength of the North Rosedale Park Civic Association was its responsiveness to residents. In response to an increase in burglaries in the Park, the organization created a safety committee in 1976, headed by William Hardin. As part of the new emphasis on safety, the committee encouraged residents to form block clubs and published safety articles each month in the *Tattler*, focusing on radio patrols, fire alarms and neighborhood watch.

As a result, block clubs formed all across the neighborhood, and

Woman's Club Bicentennial tablecloth

residents quickly learned the advantages of being organized. "Good blocks make good neighbors. We know the names and routines of each family. We have been consistently leaving our porch lights on and our block looks friendlier at night ... We have discovered each other and found it most enjoyable. We encourage all of you to discover these same things with your neighbors. You will wonder, as we do, why this did not happen a long time ago." Pat Thornton, block leader on Warwick, 1977

"We should take our hats off to the people who chose our area in the beginning: those people who never wavered when Detroit was 'under siege' in 1967, when busing became a reality, when school and city services were reduced, when unbalanced budgets and fear of crime and unrest prevailed in our city."
DONALD MYERS, NRPCA President

Neighbors in the 16800 block of Glastonbury between McNichols and Grove had a wonderful time celebrating each other in May 1975. "We think it was a great way to kick off the summer, and we plan a repeat performance sometime in September to welcome everyone back from summer vacation. We'll hope for better weather, but it seems the weather isn't as crucial as we thought: the people make the party ..." Arlene Oakland, 16821 Glastonbury

Despite the challenges facing Park residents, there were still reasons to be proud as Detroiters. "We should take our hats off to the people who chose our area in the beginning: those people who never wavered when Detroit was 'under siege' in 1967, when busing became a reality, when school and city services were reduced, when unbalanced budgets and fear of crime and unrest prevailed in our city. Those people – THESE people – are our neighbors and friends and THEY make up the backbone of our area." Donald Myers, NRPCA President, January 1977

Beth Burns, first female NRPCA president, 1979

The milestones continued. Just as the neighborhood was being integrated, so was the Civic Association. Members elected Fred Russell Sr. as a director in 1977, the first African-American on the board. The following year, Beth Burns became the first woman to be elected as vice president. Burns had previously served as the NRPCA membership secretary and would go on to become the first woman elected as NRPCA president in 1979.

"There were many high points during those 33 years (living in the Park), but my list is topped by being the first woman president of the NRPCA in 1979," Burns said. "Despite some persons' fears, NRPCA did not collapse because of a woman president. Some of the people weren't too happy, mostly men. It was the men's club where they smoked and played cards. It was a sign of the times."

Burns offered her opinion on why it took so long for the Association to admit women. "They had the Woman's Club then. So when men built the clubhouse, the women were very satisfied because the men were doing what they were told to do. When I was president, I read all of the minutes from the beginning to the end. Here was a check from a woman clipped to the minutes but was never cashed with a note from the lady wanting to be a member of the association. There was nothing in the minutes; it was never mentioned."

Burns added, "Women worked on a lot of stuff even though they weren't in the Association. We all know that we need women to get something done." A prime example of women at work, Woman's Club members were involved in numerous projects, such as providing Wayne State nursing scholarships, supporting seniors and staffing the mobile X-ray unit at Grandland. Yet not everyone knew the Club's value. "Dear Members: I am fighting mad! I have just become acquainted with a young woman who has lived in North Rosedale Park for five years. Do you know what she had been told about Rosedale Park Woman's Club? The … meetings are a competition to see who is the best dressed! Members: Will you please get out there and sell your club for what it is?" Barbara Benham

Five area associations – Rosedale Park, North Rosedale, Grandmont, Grandmont #1 and Grand River-Greenfield – formed a coalition in 1976 to address concerns about deteriorating conditions and poor customer service at Grandland Shopping Center. After meeting with the business owners, Kroger and A&P terminated open 24-hour policy, and both, along with Cunninghams, promised to undergo major remodeling; and Kroger, A&P and Great Scott promised to hire additional baggers and cashiers. In addition, the merchants formed an association, agreeing to pressure the shopping complex owners for exterior improvements, and the Detroit police mini station was relocated to Grandland to provide extra security for shoppers the following year. In a joint letter in 1977, the associations presented their plans to maintain property values in their respective areas in light of low appraisals and redlining practices.

Mr. Rosedale Contest, 1978

North Rosedale "firsts" continued to the end of the decade. Harry Gaither of Plainview was the first resident selected as the grand marshal for the 1978 June Day. An award was later named after him to recognize individuals who demonstrated a high level of commitment to North Rosedale Park. Richard Kughn, 18944 Bretton Drive, vice chairman of Taubman Company and owner of Lionel Trains, was selected as grand marshal the next year. Kughn was known for his love of antique cars and model trains, which were on display at his Carail Museum on Grand River east of Southfield.

Next came "Mr. Rosedale," a contest for the men, with women in the Park offering recommendations as to who should be considered as contestants. Each contestant had his own "canister girl," who circulated through the audience to collect votes in the form of quarters. The one with the most votes (or quarters) was declared the winner.

"They filled the Community House: the personal supporters, the curious, the nothing-better-to-dos. And by evening's end of the first annual Mr. Rosedale 1978 Contest, with the crowning of Bill Stella, Warwick, the rafters of the Community House were in jeopardy. The laughter, the hooting and howling, the whistles, the stomping – well you had to be there." The event netted more than $1,600 for the NRPCA Community Grounds fund.

Soccer players in the Rosedale Soccer League

Boy Scout Troop 123 celebrated its 50th anniversary in June 1978 with a campout on the lawn of the Community House, a free breakfast for residents and other activities. The troop was awarded a chapter on April 12, 1928, with Cooke School serving as its sponsor. Since then, thousands of young boys and fathers have been part of the troop.

In 1979, a soccer league for youth was organized by a number of Park residents, including Betty and Jim Johnson. The Johnsons, Don & Mary Scheible, and Andy & Sally Poux were joined by Phil Gorak, Mike Scott, John Baer, Joe Beaulieu, and Arnold Rzepecki as league organizers. Initially they thought they would have four or six teams and 60-90 players, but the response was 300 players.

"Almost all of the coaches and referees had no soccer background, so an enormous amount of energy went into training people as best we could," said Jim Johnson.

The Johnsons were involved with Rosedale Soccer League for about 14 years. "Many of its players continued playing on high school teams, and in all likelihood they are coaching their children in various soccer leagues today."

Focus on families and youth continued as food, babysitting and nursery school cooperatives were created to meet the needs of young families in Grandmont Rosedale. Teams did monthly food shopping at Eastern Market. Neighbors exchanged tokens for babysitting services. Nursery coops formed in local churches such as Bushnell and Calvin Presbyterian. According to Rosedale Park resident Ben Washburn, "The coops were the breeding grounds for future decades of neighborhood leaders."

The decade ended with Park residents Sarah Boyce, Mary Closson and Lisa Walters competing at the National Gymnastics Federation competition in May 1979 as members of the six-member senior modern rhythmic gymnast team. The team took first place with its group ball and ribbon routine.

North Rosedale Park Organizations

North Rosedale Park Civic Association
Association dues were used to support maintenance and upkeep of the Community House and surrounding park, which had ice rinks, two playgrounds, and a baseball diamond.

Youth Activities
- Boy Scouts and Cub Scouts
- Summer recreation program
- Fourth of July celebration
- June Day with parade, races and midway
- Ice Carnival
- Christmas Breakfast
- JA Dances

Adult Activities
- Monthly meeting with speakers from the world of business, sports, entertainment, and science
- Modern Dances
- Park Players
- Rosedale Park Bowling League
- Monthly Rosedale Tattler
- Mother's Day Breakfast
- Christmas Decorating Contest
- New Year's Eve Party

Rosedale Park Woman's Club
- Monthly meetings with a variety of speakers and entertainment
- Various activities including teas and annual luncheon
- Geriatrics Memorial Fund
- Charitable Works
- Pleasure Leisure (Seniors' Lunch)
- JA Dances
- Scholarship Program for Wayne State Nursing Students
- Community House Christmas Decorations
- House Walks

Affiliated Organizations
- Rosedale Park American Legion Post 390 and Ladies Auxiliary
- Girl Scouts

THE 1980S

The 1980s were noteworthy for so many reasons. As white flight accelerated, Detroit's white population dropped from 55 percent to 34 percent between 1970 and 1980. In the aftermath, the city faced a shrinking tax base, a glut of vacant homes, too few jobs, and increasing poverty. "Among the nation's major cities, Detroit was at or near the top of unemployment, poverty per capita, and infant mortality throughout the 1980s," according to Z'ev Chafets in an article on Detroit.[1]

Desperate to bring jobs to Detroit, Mayor Coleman Young used the power of eminent domain to purchase and raze a 465-acre area in Poletown in 1981 to make way for the GM Detroit-Hamtramck assembly plant. Originally employing 1600 workers, with a promise for more, GM announced plans to close the plant in 2019. Bowing to public pressure, GM now plans to make it the company's first plant devoted 100 percent to electric vehicles.[2]

Another major problem was crime, which landed Detroit on the FBI's list of dangerous cities way too many times. Detroit received another blow, giving new meaning to the term Devil's Night. In the mid-1980s, arson fires raged out of control, with as many as 810 fires recorded over three nights in October 1984. But by the late 1980s, Detroit began to experience a revival centered in the downtown, Midtown and New Center areas, including the renovation of the Fox Theatre and relocation of the headquarters of Little Caesars Pizza by the Ilitch family to downtown Detroit.[3]

l: NRPCA President Bill Baird and City Council President Erma Henderson chair the City Council meeting at the Community House, 1981

r: Barbara Moore (Warwick) addresses the Detroit City Council

Like prior years, North Rosedale Park could boast of having friends (and neighbors) in City government. Stina Trager managed the Far Northwest Neighborhood City Hall; Oreese Collins (Outer Drive) was named Purchasing Director by Mayor Coleman Young in 1986; and Dr. Richard Levinson (Bretton Drive) was appointed Public Health Director in 1988. City Hall came to the Park as City Council held an official community meeting in November 1981, part of a requirement to hold meetings in neighborhoods throughout the year.

The Never-Ending Fight Against Crime

Detroit's troubles couldn't help but spill over into North Rosedale Park. Like the rest of the city, the Park experienced both highs and lows. With the unemployment rate at record highs in the early 1980s and budget cuts reducing the number of police officers, property crimes increased. Despite rising crime in the northwest area, there was no increase in residential break-ins in the Park – attributed to the Park's private patrol service. "That gleaming white patrol car is a ticket to a safer neighborhood," said Officer Habkirk, 16th Precinct.

Two patrol officers with Sun National, May 1983

Like clockwork, vandalism continued – a car torched, Park Players' tents slashed, broken windows, uprooted trees, and obscenities painted on walls. The actions of the "juvenile Neanderthals" forced the Association leaders to declare that "No children will be allowed in the building except for scheduled activities, unless accompanied by a responsible adult."

Although Park residents were continually urged to support the private security patrol, it was always a struggle to get them to subscribe to the service. However, there were those who wanted the service but could not afford it. "We don't pay and our neighbors don't pay for one simple reason – we can't afford it! We can't pay $18 hoping the rate will be lowered to $13 soon, when $13 is more than we can afford. The economy just won't allow that extra expense." Debbie Orlowski, Greenview

Once again, the private security patrol was in jeopardy. By early 1983, NRPCA had contracted with a new company, Sun National Investigations & Security Systems Inc. Although the cost was similar, it took quarterly, semi-annual and annual payments and allowed sub-scribers to use credit cards. In addition, the board established a Public Safety Committee to work closely with the company to identify ways to promote the security and safety of the community. Services continued for about five years until Sun National turned over the pa-trol service to D.B. Security, a Detroit-based company.

The Public Safety Committee established a crime line in July 1984 to allow residents to leave messages if they were victims of a crime or observed suspicious activities. The com-mittee mapped the crimes to determine patterns or trends and shared the information with the 16th Precinct so that police officers could provide special surveillance. The crime line was effective. As a result of a resident's report on a suspicious car, the police trailed the car, arresting the occupants committing a robbery in the Plymouth/Evergreen area. The crime line was discontinued in 1985 to save money and eliminate prank calls.

Later that year, Park residents met with Officer Joe Golinske (16th Precinct) to organize the 90 blocks in the Park and implement the Neighborhood Watch program, a successful approach to reducing crime. The meeting was attended by 515 people, a standing-room only crowd. More than 60 people signed up for the CB Patrol, for residents to serve as "eyes and ears" to deter and report crime. Patrolling began in March. By November, the number of patrollers had jumped to 130. When Police precinct boundaries changed in 1986, the 16th Precinct became the 8th Precinct as it is today.

The Association was honored by the Detroit City Council for the work of its Safety Com-mittee in 1985 and then again two years later with its Self-Help Neighborhood Awards pro-gram. The award was given to organizations that developed self-help projects that benefited their community.

The NRPCA took an unprecedented step in 1989, signing a contract with Magnum Pri-vate Security Patrol Service to patrol the neighborhood. Rather than individual homeowners subscribing directly with the company, residents sent their monthly payments to the Asso-ciation. Pleading for support of the service, Jack O'Connell said, "Police reports have been made on all of the following: I'm talking about armed robbery ... a stolen automobile ... van-dalism ... stolen wheel covers and broken windows in an unsuccessful attempted theft. I'm talking about all of these incidents occurring all in one week – in the Park! Now is the time to support your Association, neighbors and Safety Committee by enrolling in this patrol service ... You can pay for it through your Association and have the security you need, or you can pay for it through lower real estate values but unfortunately, you will pay for it!"

Improvements at the House the Park Built

Plans to create a brick patio on the south side of the Community House were approved in July 1980, including flower beds and a 3.5-foot privacy wall built out of railroad ties and timber. The lawn was to be raised to the top of the wall with a gentle sloping hill, with shrubs, trees and flowers. The patio was built, but the wall and gentle sloping hill didn't make the cut.

Thanks to 25 Park residents, the Community House lobby got a fresh look in 1982 with volunteers removing the drop ceiling to expose the natural beams to tie in with the look in the main hall, installing six new lamps, and painting the walls and cloakrooms. A second round of improvements was completed later that year – balcony and conference room painted, two small bathrooms off the parking lot spruced up, and draperies cleaned in the main hall.

Park children had reasons to be happy as the playground was enlarged and new play equipment installed in 1984 – slide climber for toddlers, tire tree and swings, and park bench – thanks to several Park residents and Boy Scouts Curtis Schoen and Thomas Deason.

One of the signs constructed by Boy Scout Robert Gaither, 1984

Robert Gaither, another Boy Scout in pursuit of his Eagle Scout award, designed and built eight new North Rosedale Park signs that were placed at the main north and south entrances to the Park, plus two larger signs on the Community House grounds.

Gaither, Schoen and Deason all achieved Eagle Scout rank in June 1985.

Activities in the Park

A photo exhibit of Park homes called "Homes of North Rosedale" debuted at the Detroit Historical Museum and was on display for more than a month in 1982. It traced the history of North Rosedale Park since 1920 and showed the architectural character of approximately 50 homes. The significance of North Rosedale Park was the fact that it was a planned community with land set aside for a park, a concept unique for developments during that time and even today.

In 1980, the Republican National Committee held its convention in Detroit, where Ronald Reagan was nominated as the Republican candidate for president. With North Rosedale Park as home to many Republicans, the convention was attended by a number of Park residents.

Curt Samborsky won the third Mr. Rosedale Contest in 1980. Next year's winner was Bob Ruscoe. After a four-year run, the Mr. Rosedale Contest was flipped to Ms. Rosedale in 1982. More than 400 par-

Ms. Rosedale Nancy Sawyer, June Day 1983

ticipants were on hand to watch the women compete in the areas of career dress, evening dress, favorite joke, beautiful legs and talent. And the crown went to ... Nancy Sawyer.

Rosedale Soccer was such an attraction that the league had 24 teams with more than 350 players by 1982. The league games were played at the Community House field and St. Scholastica. The league was supported by the Association, St. Scholastica Parish and the American Legion Post 390.

Park residents couldn't get enough of Phil Marcus Esser, Josh White Jr. and Ron Coden, all of whom performed constantly during the decade. Esser made the first of many appearances in the Park, beginning in 1980. A dynamic singer-songwriter, director and producer, he made his mark on numerous theatrical productions around town and across the country and was credited with bringing the dinner theater concept to Detroit. He returned to perform the next year, this time with Barbara Bredius, a frequent collaborator. The duo performed five more times in the '80s. The 1984 performance at the Community House was taped by PBS and later broadcast on WTVS (Channel 56).

Back by popular demand, Josh White Jr. appeared in concert in February 1982, 1983 and 1984. During the early '80s, White spent time researching, writing and laying the groundwork for a one-man, concert-theater production simply titled *Josh*, the story of his father's life. The play debuted in 1983.

Like Esser and White, Ron Coden was a Park favorite. Coden brought his unique blend of music and comedy to the Park for concerts between 1978 and 1985. A veteran entertainer, he was dubbed a "variety show all by himself." He also appeared on the Hot Fudge Show, a children's show on WXYZ-TV.

For many years, the Association had maintained a strict policy of not being involved with politics. After some consideration, the organization decided to host Meet the Candidates Night in October 1981 to provide an opportunity for residents to hear from individuals running for office.

Association Gets to Work

The Association board constantly battled the perception that NRPCA was a clique, not open to outsiders, an image that continues until today. "What I cannot understand is this: in a community where we have over 3,000 potential members of an effective Civic Association, most of the actual work is accomplished by a couple of hundred people. If you believe that they represent a 'clique' made up of 'insiders' you are simply wrong. If you want to be involved, give any one of us a call and learn how easy it is to become an 'insider.'

Membership record for Kathy's Cakes, 1980s

"Contrary to the opinion of some, the officers and directors of the association do not constitute some sort of mini-government ... we are NRPCA members who act as a sort of collective Trustee of the resources of the Association and as a collective coordinator of activities we hope will benefit or enhance the community. The extent to which NRPCA activities benefit the entire community ... could be described as 'representation without taxation.' There is some irony in the fact that most of the people who read this ... are not NRPCA members and have elected for one reason or another not to pay the nineteen-and-one-half cents per week (19½ cents) it would cost for individual membership. Come, join the 'clique.' " Bill Baird, NRPCA President, February 1981

The Association approved a slight increase in membership fees in 1981: $25 for active and associate members; $15 for business members. Dues increased again in 1985: $35 for active and business memberships; $20 for single head of household and non-residents.

The Civic Association launched an intensive campaign to attract new members as it kicked off its "Be a Part of the Heart of North Rosedale" drive in March 1984. A group of 30 volunteers used the phones at Earl Kiem Realty to make the initial call, followed by a mailing and second call to solicit payments. Of the approximately 1700 homes in the Park, less than 500 were Civic Association members. The 318 calls resulted in 100 new memberships the next month.

Beverly Mykrantz (Glastonbury) became the first Community House manager in March 1981, a new position created by the NRPCA board. As manager and reservations secretary, she was responsible for coordinating activities at the facility; reservations and scheduling; supervision of paid personnel; and enforcement of rental contract provisions and usage rules. In late 1982, the Association announced a new manager, Joyce Heffernan (Gainsborough). When her family relocated the next year, she was replaced by Janet Kuras (Bretton) and then Chris Davis (Rosemont) in early 1985.

Beverly Mykrantz becomes the Association's first Community House manager

The block contacts (as they were called then) were invited to the monthly NRPCA meeting in April 1982 to discuss common challenges and their relationship with the Association. Organized by Beth Burns, past NRPCA President, the block contacts met again to discuss subjects like snow removal and the private patrol service.

Even with all the activity, attendance was down at Association meetings, and meetings failed to draw a quorum of at least 50 members. NRPCA President Mike Donahue expressed his frustration in 1984: "These meetings are truly our Town Hall. But do you know how many came to the three meetings combined? About 125. That's out of 6,000 people who live here … So what can we do about them? Right off hand we could cancel the meetings, or you could let the Directors know what is of interest to you and we could try another approach. Think about it, please … This is your community, not someone else's." For the rest of the decade, the Association held meetings every other month, quarterly, or as needed.

In 1989, there was a switch as the Association organized a tour of homes and gardens for the first time, in cooperation with the Woman's Club, which had sponsored it since 1965.

16710 Shaftsbury, garden walk

16823 Plainview, home tour

16190 Shaftsbury, home tour

House Walk '89 included six homes and several gardens, along with an exhibition of photograph slide sketches and watercolor drawings of Park homes, and a scavenger hunt with prizes for the winners.

The *Tattler* Tells It All

The *Rosedale Tattler* got a new editor in April 1981 as Maggie Zakem (Plainview) took over from Sally Evalt. After less than a year, Zakem resigned to spend more time with her young daughter, and Evalt was back as the editor. Kathy Nolan assumed the editor's role in 1986. For the first time that year, the *Tattler* carried a salute to Park graduates. The list included 37 eighth-graders, 34 high school graduates and one college grad.

North Rosedale Park was singled out as one of the 10 best neighborhoods in southeast Michigan by the *Metropolitan Detroit* magazine in the spring of 1984. The article pointed out some of the reasons why the neighborhood was so desirable to homebuyers. In fact, North Rosedale was the only neighborhood chosen in the city of Detroit. "It's great reading. Besides it does wonders for your self-image," said NRPCA President Mike Donahue, May 1984 *Tattler*.

Woman's Club Still at It

Like the Civic Association, the Woman's Club was an integral part of the fabric of North Rosedale Park. "We know that we no longer dress up in our hats and gloves for our regular meetings as our founding members did, but our hearts still have that common aim, which is to meet our friends and enjoy making new ones. We, each of us, should be looking to encourage our new neighbors or non-members to join the Woman's Club, for this is the only way that our new friends can know how to feel the warmth of our neighborhood, and not to feel lonely in North Rosedale Park," said Shirley O'Donnell, *Tattler* August 1983.

Karen Johnson Moore, Woman's Club President, on a Club outing in downtown Detroit.

Karen Johnson Moore, husband Columbus, and their two sons moved to Lancashire in 1981 from the Crary-St. Mary's community, where she was president. After seeing information about the Woman's Club in the *Tattler*, she thought she would go to a meeting.

"I walked there with my son in his stroller. I walked in with a navy blazer, my khakis and plaid shirt and probably some gym shoes," said Moore. Boy, was she surprised! "It was high-tea society like with my grandmother, with sterling silver service. They kind of looked at me but were polite. But I didn't get the memo. Those women were dressed in their *St. John* knits. I told my husband that I thought that I had stepped into the twilight zone."

Even after that first awkward meeting, Moore stayed engaged and became a member. "I went back because I was interested in some of the things that they were doing. I liked the idea of meeting women from other areas of the neighborhood. I found out we had something in common." She stuck around long enough to become the organization's first African-American president in 1989.

The Woman's Club wasn't exempted from societal changes, as memberships declined as women worked outside of the home and led busy lives. Moore said: "Women who are too busy for Woman's Club are my target for this year. We will be looking for ways to appeal, entertain and inform women in our area about what we do now. But more importantly, what we can do 'together' as a group of caring and aspiring women.

"I'm surprised by what I have learned about my community and, just as important, what I have learned about myself, since I have been a member of Woman's Club. I learned that it is a pleasure to meet a group of neighbors and friends in the middle of a hectic week to learn something new or just to be entertained by one of the programs. That's why I smile when someone says to me (with a sly smile on her face) 'I thought you had to wear white gloves to be a member!' I simply smile back and say, 'No. I don't own any.' "

For some, the Woman's Club was behind the times and not progressive enough. Mary Davis (Scarsdale) became a member but only for a year. Her issue was that the group still referred to women by their husband's names. "To think that in 1988 people were still being listed in the directory as Mrs. Charles L. Davis (Mary). My goodness. I am nobody's parentheses."

North Rosedale: A Community Partner

North Rosedale actively supported the Calvin Outpost, an independent organization begun in the mid-1970s and co-sponsored by North Rosedale Park, Rosedale Park, Grandmont, Grandmont #1, Schoolcraft, and Calvin Church, 14221 Southfield Road. The Outpost provided classes for all ages, including fitness, dance, calligraphy, drawing, tennis, soccer, basketball, gymnastics and karate, with six-week sessions ranging from $10 - $20.

In early 1981, the NRPCA joined the newly formed Grandgreen Business Community Association, a group of civic associations and businesses in the area bounded by Evergreen, Greenfield, Schoolcraft and McNichols. The purpose of the organization was to stem the flow of vacancies and decay in the business fronts along Grand River, McNichols, Schoolcraft, and Fenkell. A survey by the organization revealed that more than 64 million consumer dollars were spent annually by area residents out of a total income of more than $245 million. "That is one big group of geeters but, unfortunately, not enough of it is spent here. Yet. We hope to coax more of these dollars to remain here ... So listen since it's all for us, what would it hurt if we got a little help from you? How? It's obvious: Shop Grandgreen." Bill Baird, NRPCA President, July 1981

With the proliferation of for sale signs in northwest Detroit, the four area community organizations reached an agreement with 12 realty companies to place a moratorium on for sale signs. The ban began in April 1985.

Boulevard Florist and Greenhouse, 19600 Grand River, and Gordon Williamson Co., 19180 Grand River, location of the Neighborhood City Hall and later Always Brewing and Town Hall Caffé coffee shops

In a letter to *Crain's Detroit Business* in January 1987, NRPCA President Don Scheible wrote: "The real estate article of January 5, 1987 ('Location, Location, Location – Agents say site, not size determines housing prices') presented an interesting comparison of existing housing in the metro Detroit area. We were told that proximity to industrial land uses (Woodhaven), open spaces (Canton), rural quality (Shelby Township) and prestige (Birmingham/Beverly Hills) are keys in determining the value of property. However, we are also told that value in Detroit, or at least the Rosedale Park area, is determined by Race, Race, Race and not Location, Location, Location. It is certainly a disgrace and a tragedy that race has been, is now and will likely be a primary factor in establishing the listing price, appraised value and insurability of homes in our area and other places where Black families choose to live in pursuit of their dreams ... we invite those who seek unparalleled value and quality in their home, who crave a uniquely cohesive community, who long for an excellent place to raise their children and who don't care what color their neighbor's skin is as long as they're a good neighbor, to come visit Rosedale Park. Fortunately, true value cannot be measured in terms of location."

In response to the same article, Freman Hendrix (Bretton) expressed his astonishment at "blatantly racist" statements made by Don Wilson, broker and owner of Earl Keim Rosedale Realty about the drop in housing values because of Blacks moving into the area. "If one were to do his or her homework (and apparently Mr. Wilson didn't do his), it wouldn't take any Albert Einstein to understand that economics and quality of life in a community are what impact real estate values. Factors, such as the cost of living (taxes), the local school system, and crime (both real and perceived), are what good people are concerned with, not the color of their neighbor's skin. So we extend an invitation to all to visit and make this fine community your home and discover what good neighbors are all about!"

Staying Put

In the wake of so many families leaving Detroit, residents from the four Grandmont Rosedale neighborhoods – Rosedale Park, Grandmont, Grandmont #1 and North Rosedale Park – formed a group called "The Stayers." The name denoted the group's purpose: to encourage residents to **stay** in Detroit. The group, formally called Grandmont Rosedale Integrated Neighborhoods, started with frank conversations with neighbors at house meetings.

"It kind of freaked us out as our friends started to leave. I thought we had to do something about that," said Mary Sue Schottenfels, who formed the group in 1987 with her husband, Dr. Frank Lanzilote. They had moved to Grandmont #1 in 1979 because it was integrated. "We wanted people to talk about why they had come here in the first place and what was needed to help them stay. There were so many (for sale) signs in the neighborhood. And we thought that was not stabilizing things. This was a counterweight to that. It wasn't about keeping white people; it was about keeping the neighborhood stable and keeping people from leaving."

Come Live the Dream billboard, Grandmont Rosedale Integrated Neighborhoods (The Stayers), 1988

The group included a number of families: Frey, Goodman, Halloran, Moore, LePere-Schloop, Regalado/Schottenfels, Tupper, Blaum/Wilbur, Soisson, Christo, Bitzarakis, Hendrix, Gay, Stallworth and many others. As a means to promote Grandmont Rosedale, it organized the first neighborhood open house in 1988 to showcase homes for sale and educate realtors on the area's advantages. The open house drew 400 individuals and 70 realtors with a second one planned for the following year. Other activities included Martin Luther King dinners with speakers and picnics, and billboards promoting its theme: "Come Live the Dream." "The events that we had attracted new people to the area," Lanzilote added. "It gave people a feel of the neighborhoods."

In an open letter to residents of Rosedale Park and the city in September 1987, Chris and Ruth Remus (Warwick) wrote: "Recently, we put our beloved Rosedale Park home up for sale. We had two 'incidents' at our house and we were just tired of the hassles of break-ins, purse snatchings, stolen bikes and more. But our house didn't sell right away and we've had time to rethink the process. The recent Fr. Cunningham talk, the stories about guns and knives in suburban schools also, the commitment to live in an integrated area, the efforts of 8th Precinct Inspector Vasiloff to decrease crime in our neighborhood and the quality of our home and the neighbors with which we live, caused us to change our minds. We feel that even with the problems that we know exist here, as they do in every other community, this is where we fit best. This is where 'The Dream is (still) alive despite the world of difference.' And also where we white folks can still feel like we belong here. Rosedale Park and the city of Detroit, we love you too much to leave. And as we reverse the trend of flight to the suburbs, we join a unique group. We too, will now be known as 'Stayers.' "

While the work of the Stayers generated a number of positive stories, there was one negative story in particular that upset a lot of Park residents. Susan Ager, *Detroit Free Press* reporter, did a rather lengthy story on residents on one block of Rosemont in 1988. The response to the story was swift and triggered multiple letters to the *Free Press* and *Tattler* editors.

Loyce Turpin (Rosemont) convinced her neighbors to be interviewed, but was extremely disappointed in the final story. "The article that came out ended up feeling more focused on lack of hope than presence of it ... If anything, it united us for a period of time, but I felt really responsible for stirring that up at the time since pride in the neighborhood had been my motive for participating."

A letter from Grandmont Rosedale Integrated Neighborhoods and signed by 152 individuals expanded on those feelings. " 'Park People' examines in detail the real problems of real people living on one block in North Rosedale Park. As residents of the Grandmont Rosedale community in northwest Detroit, we grapple with those problems every day ... We also know, from our own experience, that there is another side to the story. There was a spirit that exists in these neighborhoods that the article failed to capture ... Fourteen months ago, a handful of residents in our community came together to renew their commitment to stay. Since that time, this informal network of 'stayers' has grown to include hundreds of families. A spirit of pride, determination and joy is alive in this neighborhood. That is the story that needs to be told."

That kind of pride and determination was evident when a group of Park residents led by John O'Brien and Morris Goodman founded the North Rosedale Non-Profit Development Corporation (NRNDC) in 1989 to help stabilize the neighborhood through renovating homes. O'Brien, Goodman and Pastor William Kight of Calvin Presbyterian Church pulled together residents of the four neighborhood associations that had already envisioned the creation of the Grandmont Rosedale Development Corporation (GRDC) to focus on purchasing and renovating blighted homes. With this is mind, O'Brien prepared and submitted

15894 Ashton, first house renovated by North Rosedale Non-Profit Development Corporation

a grant application to the State of Michigan Neighborhood Builder's Alliance program to finance the creation of the North Rosedale Non-Profit Development Corporation.

Governor James Blanchard was on hand in January 1989 to announce that the NRPCA had received the $55,000 State grant to renovate and resell residential homes in the Park, address safety-related projects, and promote Cooke School and beautify its grounds. Those funds were turned over to NRNDC and used to rehab 15894 Ashton, with the newly formed GRDC hired to manage the project. The home was purchased for $9,000, with $46,000 in renovations, including siding and new garage, kitchen and bathroom improvements, and plumbing and electrical updates. After several years of working with GRDC, NRNDC was dissolved and its limited assets were turned over to GRDC to continue the home renovation work.

The Grandmont Rosedale Development Corporation was also initially funded by a $55,000 Builder's Alliance grant. Subsequent funding came from a multi-year grant by the Local Initiatives Support Corporation (LISC), yearly donations from the four neighborhood associations, banks and other corporations, and donations from neighborhood residents. John O'Brien was the first executive director, followed by Tom Goddeeris (Rosemont) in 1991. In 2017, Goddeeris moved on to Detroit Future City, and Sherita Smith became GRDC's third executive director.

GRDC's impact is impressive. By its 10th anniversary in 1999, it had renovated 31 vacant homes; assisted 33 homeowners with grants and loans for home repairs; eliminated graffiti through work with Graffiti Busters; planted 60 new trees along McNichols; helped build new playgrounds in North Rosedale Park and at Cooke School; and organized similar efforts at Flintstone Park, Ramsey Park, Stoepel Park and Vetal Elementary School. By 2020, GRDC's accomplishments included: 120 single-family homes renovated; three new homes built and sold to low/moderate income families; home repair loans and grants to 156 homeowners; renovation of five commercial buildings; helping several small businesses get funding and open in the neighborhood; helping 38 business owners redo their storefronts through a Commercial Façade Improvement Program; opening the first neighborhood co-working space at Grand River Workplace; and establishing the Farmers' Market, the first of its kind outside of the Eastern Market.

Not surprisingly, GRDC gained a reputation for being an effective and well-run organization. "I think that one of the strengths of GRDC was not having to focus on one neighborhood. If each neighborhood tried to start its own group, it wouldn't have worked," said Goddeeris, who served as executive director for 26 years. "One of the strengths of the organization is being able to bring all the neighborhoods together."

Bill Frey, a Park resident and GRDC board member for more than 30 years, also appreciates its impact. "It has been amazing what this grassroots organization has been able to accomplish since it started in 1989," Frey said. "Anyone who knows what is going on with neighborhood development in Detroit will tell you that GRDC has been and remains one of the most effective organizations in the city."

Is There Racism in the Park?

That was the question posed by Kathy Nolan to *Tattler* readers after a rather sensitive situation between neighbors played out for the entire neighborhood to see in 1989. A group of 45 neighbors sent a letter to neighbors Lawson and Grant on official NRPCA stationery (unauthorized by the Association) regarding basketball games in the street that attracted up to 20 young people and created excessive noise, thereby destroying "the general peace and quiet of our part of this fine neighborhood." They asked that the basketball hoops on the garages be removed by Saturday, May 20, 1989.

Roger and Mary Lawson, a Caucasian couple, responded with a letter to the *Tattler* editor, a portion of which read: "Many of you are known to us by name. Many are neighbors we have worked with on school, church and civic activities. Several of you have been entertained in our home. Yet not one of you has approached our family personally to discuss concerns you may be experiencing with the use of basketball hoops on our street. None of you called to let us know our family was being discussed at a civic association board meeting, a letter being composed and a door-to-door signature campaign conducted. It appears that the initiator(s) of this letter has been selling his/her/their philosophy on the "evils of neighborhood basketball" block by block and anonymously in the *Tattler* as well. Is this the kind of community spirit North Rosedale Park prides itself on? Our family is deeply shocked and offended by this unneighborly conduct.

"There is one factor that has changed over the past couple of years ... and that is the majority of boys who gather at our garage are no longer white. Is it a coincidence that the majority of the kids congregating at the side of our house are black and the majority of the names on this letter are white? Is it hypocritical to invite people to "come live the dream" in North Rosedale Park when a gathering of black youth appears to be so offensive and threatening to so many? Many of these young people you refer to as "total strangers" are, in fact, your neighbors too. The Hoop Stays.

"We have met with our neighbors to set further rules and regulations for this year's 'playing season.' We invite suggestions and assistance from any of you who are interested in sitting down with us, neighbor to neighbor, to discuss this matter."

Several residents responded to Nolan's question of whether there was racism in the Park. Most said yes. "Of course there is racism in Rosedale Park. This is a marvelous place to live, but it is not heaven, so there is sin. I am concerned how we react to any comment that there is racism. This defensiveness, I believe, indicates that there is a festering sore and there may be a need for some real soul-searching, admittance, conversation or workshops. I was saddened by the letter circulated. It showed, I believe, our inability to communicate (talk face-to-face), if what was written was correct. I don't think we should have to be mind readers. What bothers others may not bother me at all, and unless I'm told, I'll never know it." Liz Sturkol

In Other Park News

American Legion Post 390 got its own home in 1981 by purchasing the former Sno-White restaurant building, 18944 Grand River. Post 390 had rented the Community House and made significant contributions to its upkeep and improvements over the years. The Fresenius Medical Care now occupies the building.

North Rosedale Park residents benefited when the Redford Branch Library, 21200 Grand River, opened in 1981.

THE 1990S

The decade of the 1990s was a period of monumental developments across the country and the world. But what is a decade without a military conflict? Iraq under Saddam Hussein invaded Kuwait in 1990, triggering the Persian Gulf War. South Africa repealed apartheid in 1991, paving the way for Nelson Mandela as the country's first Black president. Eastern European communist regimes fell; East and West Germany were reunited; the USSR was dismantled; and the European Union was formed.

At home, the 1995 Oklahoma City bombing, the deadliest domestic terrorism attack in U.S. history, killed 168 people and injured more than 680. That same year, millions of African-American men converged on Washington, DC for the Million Man March.

Locally, Detroit's population stood at 1,027,974. The decade witnessed the killing of Malice Green (28 years before George Floyd); demolition of the Hudson's building; the assisted suicide crusade of Dr. Jack Kevorkian; and a 1995 strike against Detroit's two daily newspapers which lasted nearly two years.

NRPCA Working Cooperatively

The 1990s began with a successful effort by the NRPCA and area community organizations to stop the sale of the Burtha M. Fisher Home for the Aged and Poor, at the Southfield service drive and W. Outer Drive, to Job Corps. The home had opened in 1928 and closed in 1989. Plans called for the facility to be renovated to house and train approximately 280 youth, some with troubled backgrounds. Although Mayor Coleman A. Young supported the plan, the Civic Association was able to secure Michigan Governor James Blanchard's veto of the site for the Job Corps. Five years later, the NRPCA and the other organizations celebrated the opening of the College Park Commons shopping center anchored by a Farmer Jack grocery store and Henry Ford Health System on the site.

Residents of the big four neighborhood associations – North Rosedale Park, Rosedale Park, Grandmont and Grandmont #1 – came together the next year to develop an action plan

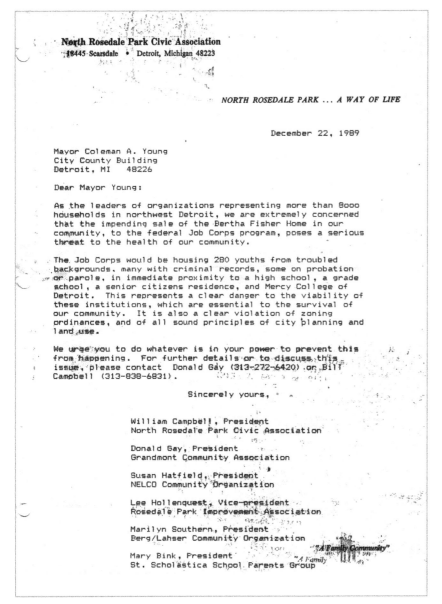

NRPCA appeals to Mayor Young regarding Burtha Fisher site

Text within the letter image:

North Rosedale Park Civic Association
18445 Scarsdale • Detroit, Michigan 48223

NORTH ROSEDALE PARK ... A WAY OF LIFE

December 22, 1989

Mayor Coleman A. Young
City County Building
Detroit, MI 48226

Dear Mayor Young:

As the leaders of organizations representing more than 8000 households in northwest Detroit, we are extremely concerned that the impending sale of the Bertha Fisher Home in our community, to the federal Job Corps program, poses a serious threat to the health of our community.

The Job Corps would be housing 280 youths from troubled backgrounds, many with criminal records, some on probation or parole, in immediate proximity to a high school, a grade school, a senior citizens residence, and Mercy College of Detroit. This represents a clear danger to the viability of these institutions, which are essential to the survival of our community. It is also a clear violation of zoning ordinances, and of all sound principles of city planning and land use.

We urge you to do whatever is in your power to prevent this from happening. For further details or to discuss this issue, please contact Donald Gay (313-272-6420) or Bill Campbell (313-838-6831).

Sincerely yours,

William Campbell, President
North Rosedale Park Civic Association

Donald Gay, President
Grandmont Community Association

Susan Hatfield, President
NELCO Community Organization

Lee Hollenquest, Vice-president
Rosedale Park Improvement Association

Marilyn Southern, President
Berg/Lahser Community Organization

Mary Bink, President
St. Scholastica School Parents Group

"A Family Community"

---

for the area focusing on housing, schools, safety and commercial strips. Following a neighborhood forum with 120 residents, participants formed committees to initially focus on the Grandland Shopping Center and area schools – Vetal, Edison and Cooke. The Grandland committee's recommendations centered on appearance and safety at the center. The education task force narrowed its focus to working with local school community organizations, area associations and the Detroit school board to enhance student achievement and reinvest in area youth.

"Help save the Outpost" was the plea in the June 1991 *Tattler*. The program sponsored by the four neighborhood associations and Calvin Presbyterian Church had experienced a decline in participation from more than 500 participants in the mid-70s to 150 in 1991. The Outpost got a new home at St. Timothy United Methodist Church on Archdale and Puritan. The move was necessary as Calvin Presbyterian Church, which had provided 35 years of service to the Grandmont Rosedale area, merged with Westminster Presbyterian Church on Hubbell near Outer Drive in April 1994.

The Business of the Association

The Association faced a tough decision in 1990 when the paper for the *Tattler* was noticeably inferior to that used for previous issues, having been downgraded by the printer because of financial constraints. In response, the Association contracted with a new publisher, thereby ending its 65-year relationship with The Redford Printing Company at 17205 Lahser. The change in publishing companies also meant the Association was responsible for securing ads.

In early 1991, Sally Evalt again took over as *Tattler* editor from Kathy Nolan, who served for five years. Mary Ratkowski (Sunderland) was named *Tattler* editor in January 1994 followed by Sharon LeMieux.

Delphine and Leon Tupper

North Rosedale made history once again as Delphine Tupper was elected as the first African American president of the Association in 1991. "I felt the weight of it. I felt that being the first of anything that you had to be less flawed," Tupper said. "I thought I was an example to bring more Black people in. After me, you can see more Black people were elected."

Her tenure, unfortunately, was not without its challenges. "I believe that my agenda was undercut by people, although I had supported others' agendas." Tupper said she also received calls from individuals complaining about their Black neighbors not knowing that she was Black. Despite that, Tupper said she felt embraced and included with all the other past presidents.

As was the case in prior decades, the Association constantly challenged residents to join the organization, volunteer and attend events, but the majority simply didn't. In 1991, memberships stood at 683 out of 1700 households, meaning that only 40 percent of households were members. "In a city where failed, neglected neighborhoods abound, North Rosedale Park is a shining example to all of what neighborhood solidarity and gumption can accomplish ... The $35 membership fee is a very small investment to protect a very important asset – the vitality of the neighborhood where many have chosen to live and raise their families." (Membership article in *Rosedale Tattler*, November 1991)

Association leaders returned to scheduling monthly membership meetings after hearing complaints in 1990. Yet, at times, attendance was poor. "I remember hearing all those complaints about not having general meetings ... The reason previous boards have not had general meetings was for this very reason, very poor attendance. It is not fair to our speakers." Association President Christine Davis, June 1990

Chris Allen, 1992 Association President, shared similar sentiments after attending a Martin Luther King celebration. "I walked away from the celebration rejoicing because in North Rosedale Park we are living the dream that King worked to achieve – a community where whites and blacks, old and young, live as one community and support a philosophy that King spoke of often. In our community we are blessed, and sometimes we take it for granted. There are communities not far from North Rosedale, which are totally isolated and segregated. Let us all take time out of our schedules, and make a commitment to keeping this community strong."

President Jim Johnson said it again in 1994. "The proverb, 'It takes a whole village to raise a child,' is true, but it isn't all that easy to carry out. It means that you have to recognize the importance of your immediate neighborhood to passing on your values, and you'll have to get involved in the process." People must have heeded what Johnson said about the importance of membership. The Association recorded 886 members in October 1994, the most in ten years.

The membership considered key changes to its constitution in 1995 including narrowing memberships to four categories (active, non-resident, life and honorary); allowing non-resident members to hold appointed offices; requiring that the Association's income or property would not be used to benefit members, officers, or private individuals; requiring its assets to go to the City of Detroit if the Association was dissolved; adopting a schedule of a January annual meeting with general membership meetings in April, September and December; increasing the number of directors by one to a total of seven; and providing for removal of officers and directors for missing board meetings and appointed officers for failing to perform their duties.

But before any vote, the opposition began lobbying. Major points of contention were allowing non-residents to serve as appointed officers and distribution of assets if the Association was dissolved. A past president wrote to the *Tattler* editor; another resident told members to vote no. In the end, all amendments were approved except one – the proposal to add Assistant Treasurer to the title of the Reservation Secretary.

Lyle and Louise Reading

The board also dealt with the problem of rising costs of activities and maintaining the Community House and park. Dues increased from $35 to $40 in 1996.

The Civic Association honored two longtime members – Van Darsey and Lyle Reading – who represented the commitment to keeping the community strong. Darsey and his late wife, Loraine, moved to North Rosedale Park in 1936, seeking to live where there were open spaces. Darsey, an Association member for 60 years, recalled that when he looked out from his porch, he saw cornfields on one side and weeds on the other. Reading, a 56-year member, lived in his childhood home on Lancashire with his wife, Louise. He was part of the second graduating class at Cooke School and participated in the first June Day parade in 1930, playing the trumpet for the Redford District Band. He was elected to the Civic Association board several times and served as the North Rosedale Park historian and archivist. Both men were designated as grand marshals for the June Day celebration in 1996.

Continuing its tradition of attracting noted leaders, the Association invited Dennis Archer, the newly elected mayor, to serve as the grand marshal for June Day in 1994.

Mayor Dennis Archer, Grand Marshal, and Congressman John Conyers participate in June Day parade

l-r: Jim Johnson, Mayor Archer and Bill Frey

The Park in the Spotlight

The family of George and Margaret Ward (Bretton Drive) made it to the big screen as extras in the film, *Presumed Innocent*, starring Harrison Ford in 1990. Ford had shadowed George Ward earlier to understand the role of a prosecuting attorney, which George played for real for Wayne County. The film was about a prosecutor who needed to clear himself after he was charged with murder. It was shot in 1989 and was the latest in a string of movies filmed entirely or partially in Detroit, which included *Beverly Hills Cop I & II, American Cops*

I & II, *The Rosary Murders*, and *An American Beauty*. The Ward family appeared three times in the movie.

ABC News *Primetime Live* did a feature story on Detroit in 1990 that contained a brief reference to North Rosedale Park and footage of Park residents dancing at the Steak Roast. Reporter Judd Rose focused on the city's challenges with blight, crime, drugs, Devil's Night fires, and poverty. By many accounts, the story was a "hatchet job" and lacked balanced

Actor Harrison Ford with Park resident and attorney George Ward

reporting. Others criticized Mayor Coleman Young for using colorful language during his interview.

"Primetime was a disappointment to say the least. Park residents had a vested interest in the program because we thought we would be featured. Well, we were; but I hope no one blinked," said Kathy Nolan, December 1990 *Tattler*. "I have no illusions that Detroit is perfect; but it's the place in which I have chosen to raise my children and they have benefited for all they have learned by living here (both good and bad). I'm sorry that the news people

ABC News *PrimeTime Live*

from New York felt they had...to sensationalize the story and take advantage of people who trusted them; but I'm glad that Mayor Young didn't roll over and play dead to their music."

Mayor Coleman Young responded to Nolan's letter. "Your editorial reflected the outrage that was felt by many Detroiters when ABC aired its hatchet job. I particularly enjoyed your speculation about the way your grandfather, Joe Martin, would have handled a similar situation when he was mayor. He

sounds like quite a man, someone I would have enjoyed knowing. Again thank you for your words of support."

John O'Connell Jr. had a similar view but from a different angle. He believed the program was slanted, but also felt Detroit needed a wake-up call. "I'm glad that you distorted the picture because there are a lot of problems in Detroit, just as there are in many big cities. I think you might have gotten the public's attention enough to do something about it."

Although crime had become a constant source of stress and occurred all too often for

Park residents, nothing could have prepared them for the news of the murder of Andre Poux, a Civic Association board member, in his Shaftsbury home in November 1990. His murder rocked the community, with some residents packing up and moving out of the city. News reports indicated that Poux went downstairs to investigate a noise and was shot in the chest by intruders.

Close friend George Ward met Poux in 1960 when they attended the University of Detroit. He shared these words at Poux's funeral. "I enjoyed 30 years of friendship and laughter with Andy, and now I've found myself thinking if the next 30 years will bring as much warmth and laughter … but aren't such things an inappropriate way to remember a man who was such a bright light? Andy laughed because he loved life and found humor in it. He wanted us to find it, too. It's still there. We'll best honor his memory if we are alert to it, as he always was." The Wards left North Rosedale after Poux's death. Two men were convicted of his murder in 1991.

Andre Poux

Poux's murder led to a renewed effort to address crime in the Park. Board member Pete Logan said, "Crime is a reality in the metropolitan Detroit area, and recent incidents, including the tragic death of our friend, Andy Poux, reminds us that one of the area's best neighborhoods is not excluded from the reality of crime … We've chosen to live in the Park because we want to live with people who pull together to solve problems. And together we can take a stand against crime and restore the sense of security we all desire in our community."

Association leaders and the Public Safety Committee once again urged residents to join the CB patrol and to support the private security patrol. NRPCA President Delphine Tupper, however, expressed her disappointment at the lack of turnout for public safety projects in the Park. "Our Public Safety Committee has worked very hard this year to make North Rosedale one of the safest communities in Michigan (not just Detroit) to live in. A safe neighborhood seems to be what everyone wants. Right? … I'll climb down off my soapbox if you promise to get involved. Remember, if we don't do it ourselves, no one else will."

Unfortunately, those appeals fell on deaf ears. The patrol service provided by Magnum Security Services was reduced from 60 to 42 hours a week in February 1992 because of declining subscriptions. Same song, same verse.

Two years later, another murder in the Park sparked anger and resulted in changes to the Community House rental policy. In January 1993, a young man was shot and later died after a 16th birthday party at the Community House. The incident started with a fight inside the facility, with the offending parties being escorted out of the party. The police arrived, and things seemed to settle down. One of those individuals later returned with a gun and shot the young man. In response to the fatal shooting, the Civic Association instituted new rules limiting rentals for youth events to NRPCA members and subject to board approval, and making contracted security services mandatory for all rentals.

In response to reports of robberies at area homes and businesses, and car jackings that year, Association President Freman Hendrix appointed a crime summit steering committee in 1993 to develop action plans focused on community resources, and scheduled a crime summit for November.

At the crime summit, attended by more than 300 residents, subcommittees decided to focus on three areas: security patrol, CB patrol, and lighting and traffic control. The security patrol committee recommended a new vendor, D'Mar Security Patrol Services. The CB patrol committee recommended making the patrol a NRPCA-owned entity; operating two vehicles on two weeknights from 7-11 p.m.; completing Police Department training; acquiring equipment; and identifying a professional coordinator. The lighting and traffic control committee's recommendations included requesting additional street signs; prohibiting on-street parking between 2 to 6 a.m.; increasing police presence; and reducing the number of access points to the Park and through streets by focusing on one-way streets and street closures.

Over the years, North Rosedale contracted with a number of security companies: Magnum Security Services in the early 1990s; D'Mar Security Patrol Services in 1994; Imperial Security in 1995; Great Lakes Protection Service in 1996; and Pinkerton Security Service in 1997. While residents' support of patrol services was sporadic, Association leaders could point to the effectiveness of the patrols in averting crime.

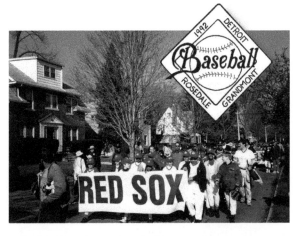

Rosedale-Grandmont Baseball League Opening Day Parade

Engaging Park Youth

The 1990s saw an explosion of activities for youth. In 1992, a group of residents from the big four neighborhoods started the Rosedale-Grandmont Baseball and Softball League for children starting at age five. Freman Hendrix began looking for a baseball program for his son, Stephen, then around 4 or 5 years old. He and other parents entered a team in a Livonia league. "We saw 2-3 other teams from the area in that league," said

Hendrix, one of the league organizers. "So we thought we should form our own league."

The core group – Frank Lanzilote, Ken Schneider, Cheryl Montgomery, Brenda Martin and Elaine and Freman Hendrix – met at Hendrix's home and mapped out the league. "We were so nervous when we started," Hendrix said. "We needed 100 kids or thereabout to have enough to start the league. We had 150 boys and girls that came out. We didn't get anything from the City or sponsors; it was all built on the strength of the parents." By the second season, the league had grown to more than 450 players.

A similar response occurred with the formation of the Rosedale-Grandmont Youth Basketball League for boys and girls, ages 6-12. The league began its first season in October 1993 with roughly 200 participants. "We just wanted to provide a safe, clean environment where

Hornets team, Rosedale-Grandmont Youth Basketball League

kids could just have a good time without the pressure to win," said Leslie Martin, who organized the league with her husband, Ray. "And it is still done with parent volunteers." The league operated for 15 years.

North Rosedale received a 2-for-1 offer in 1992, one that would benefit both the neighborhood and Park resident Greg Hall with his studies at the University of Michigan. Earlier, Hall had discussed plans with Association leaders to raise funds for playground equipment damaged during a storm in 1991. Then when he was required to do a community project for a graduate class, he immediately presented the Park playground project. "This is an immediate community need the group can get excited about, and one

I'm familiar enough with to help out. When I suggested this as a possible class project, five people offered to be a part of the effort. The timing was just perfect!" Hall also saw the project as a great way to expose others to the good things happening in Detroit. The hard work of the U-M group, block captains and area residents came to fruition as new playground equipment was installed that year.

The Community House playground got additional attention as a newly formed playground committee spent several days in 1997

Park residents, including the kids, celebrate the playground dedication, 1998

repairing playground equipment, giving it a fresh coat of paint and spreading sand. However, the group had bigger plans – raise $90,000 to redo the entire playground. Committee members were elated with a donation of $27,600 from Frank Stella and his family. Stella, a resident of 50 years, was active in the Association and a successful entrepreneur with a restaurant supply company. The playground was named in honor of Stella's wife and son – Martha T. and Daniel F. Stella Memorial Playground. By July 1998, the committee had raised $90,868, exceeding its goal. The North Rosedale Park community dedicated the new playground in October 1998.

Since the earliest days of the Woman's Club, JA (Junior Activities) dances were held for Park teens, a tradition that continued in the 1990s. Now sponsored by the Civic Association, the dances were held four times a year to provide an opportunity for young people to meet and to have fun through dancing and socializing.

Players Still Providing Quality Productions

Park Players celebrated its 40th anniversary at the Community House in September 1993. As successful as it was, however, the troupe was finding it difficult to cast and produce plays with just Park residents who were NRPCA members.

"Unless there is a resurgence in Park residents, past and present, getting and staying involved in Players, the organization will probably have to open the boundaries to those who can be members in order to survive. This will, in a short time, I believe, make Players just another theater group as opposed to an important part of what makes North Rosedale work as a community. Please don't let this happen," said Players' member Morris Goodman, May 1992 *Tattler*.

Park Players celebrate 40th anniversary with hit musical *The King and I*, 1993

In the early 1990s, Park Players allowed members from surrounding associations to join. The troupe again revised its by-laws in 1996 to add a non-resident membership to allow anyone to join the group.

Like Goodman, Sally Evalt, the *Tattler* editor, had a growing concern with the lack of residents' participation in activities. "There's a growing, knowing feeling within me ... that the feeling of COMMUNITY is slowly deteriorating in North Rosedale. June Day, for instance, was a wonderful day for those adults and children who participated during the daylong activities. But what about the hundreds of Park residents who chose to ignore the event altogether.

"Even on my street, where once each new birth was celebrated up and down the block, I see some signs of 'neighborly' decline. This neighborhood didn't become a 'good' neighborhood by accident. Plenty of hard work – all volunteered time – on the part of thousands of residents over the past 60 years has kept North Rosedale Park one of the premier neighborhoods in the state. Now more than ever we need each resident's resolve to get involved, and to do his/her share to continue the activities and programs which have set this neighborhood apart from those Detroit neighborhoods which have decayed."

Evalt backed up those words in the case of Mary Davis and her family. Davis was involved in a serious car accident and was hospitalized for 1½ months. Evalt organized Park Players members to provide dinner for the family. "For over two months now, friends and neighbors in Park Players have been taking turns bringing dinner almost every night of the week," said Davis. "Doctors and nurses were always impressed when they inquired about the boys and were told about the dinners. 'You must live in a terrific neighborhood,' they would say. I assured them that I most certainly did." Mary Davis, 1995

Larry and Chris Davis, both past NRPCA presidents, with their sons, Todd, Justin and Matthew, in June Day parade, 1999

Children watch a puppet show by the Detroit Recreation Department during Westmoreland block party, 1990

North Rosedale Park Civic Association website

Lots to Celebrate!

It was a good decade in many respects, with GRDC receiving its largest grant of $466,600 from the State of Michigan for improvements in Rosedale Park and Minock Park; creation of a Boulevard Flower Bed Matching Fund by NRPCA to encourage residents to plant and maintain flower beds in the Park; formation of the youth sports leagues; and the start of Rosedale Recycles by the Rosedale Park Improvement Association in April 1990. It was the city's first recycling center on the west side.

There was more good news when the Repair the Roof project raised enough funds in 1995 to replace the roof on the Community House at a cost of $22,300. The NRPCA made its debut on the World Wide Web in July 1995 with a new website that provided information on activities, the neighborhood and organization. The NRPCA was out in front in terms of technological advances. It would be another three years before the City of Detroit announced it had a website. The website has since gone through many revisions.

It was a special time for the Woman's Club as well. A group of 80 women, some driving in from Florida, celebrated the 75th anniversary of the Club with a luncheon at the Com-

Woman's Club 75th Anniversary Luncheon

Woman's Club past presidents

munity House on May 8, 1999. The celebration included 14 past presidents and honored two long-standing members – Louise Reading, a member for 50 years, and Elsie Master, a 25-year member.

Margaret Cowley commemorated the event with a poem, "Yesteryear, Now and Forever."

Woman's Club luncheon, 75th Anniversary

A Club for women only was formed in '23
The "Woman's Club of Rosedale" was our Society –
Lunches, meetings, parties, tours,
Were all a SPECIAL date.
Members proudly worked and planned
To make these functions Great!

Years have passed, some lifestyles changed,
Our membership is low,
Dedicated women have kept our club "Aglow",
"Woman's Club of Rosedale", A Special Club Indeed,
Commemorates a milestone, joint efforts Did succeed.

Let's celebrate our birthday, A Diamond Jubilee,
And, THANKS TO ALL who made this day
A happy memory.

Over the years, the Woman's Club had made numerous contributions to the Association for various projects and initiatives. In 1998, the Club donated a new commercial gas stove with ten burners and two ovens to the Association for the Community House, which was quickly put to use for June Day.

Like many organizations, membership had dropped in recent years as lifestyles changed. Club leaders sought to develop a strategic plan to move the Club into the new millennium, with assistance from Suzanne Heath, a professional facilitator from Catholic Youth Organization.

The decade ended with Park residents and the entire world waiting anxiously to see if Y2K would usher in interruptions and the collapse of the technology infrastructure. It didn't.

THE 2000S

The decade of the 2000s is easily defined as a period of triumphs and tragedies. The tragedies were devastating, including the terrorist attacks in New York, Washington, DC and Pennsylvania on 9/11; the great recession brought on by the housing and mortgage crisis in the United States; and Hurricane Katrina, which devastated New Orleans and other parts of Louisiana and Mississippi in 2005. Yet, the decade is also remembered for the big blackout which left roughly 55 million people in eight U.S. states and a portion of Canada in the dark for a couple of days in 2003.

As for the triumphs, there was the historic election of Barack Obama as the first Black U.S. president in 2008, and the introduction of technology that dramatically changed how Americans communicated – Facebook (2004), Twitter (2006) and the iPhone (2007).

Locally, sports played a big role as the Pistons were NBA champs in 2004; Detroit hosted Major League Baseball's All-Star Game in 2005 and the Super Bowl XL in 2006; and the Tigers made it to the World Series in 2006 but lost.

On a sad note, the nation mourned the death of civil rights icon Rosa Parks in 2005, and Detroiters lamented the resignation of Detroit Mayor Kwame Kilpatrick in 2008.

Here in the Park, the leaders of the Rosedale Park Woman's Club announced the end of an era, as the organization dissolved in 2000. The decision was not an easy one, but inevitable, after attempts to revitalize the organization and attract new members came up short. "When the women weren't working they could do things like have tea in the afternoon," said Marcia Closson, a former Woman's Club vice president. "When women got into the workforce, it was hard to get new members to join. Most of the women in the Park were working or they were old." Chris Davis, the last Woman's Club president, agreed. "With most members on average in their 70s, no one was interested in running for the board. We had meetings upon meetings. We tried to make it one more year. No one was really interested in keeping it alive."

The group held a final spring luncheon in May and divided its items – tablecloths, teapots, silver-plated spoons and platters – among remaining members. Closson was disappointed with the Club ending. "It was a sad thing because it was really fun. It had been around for such a long, long time." Not wanting to lose touch with each other, members of the Woman's Club met the following year for a reunion luncheon.

The History of Detroit and the Park

Although the Woman's Club ended, June Day – a tradition since 1930 – continued. Over the years, June Day organizers could boast of some noted grand marshals. Mayor Dennis Archer was grand marshal in 1994. June Day 2000 had three grand marshals: Frank Stella, a longtime Park resident and major donor to the Community House playground; Frankie Dar-cell, WJLB radio personality; and Rich Fisher, Channel 50 news anchor. The grand marshal for June Day 2001 was Roman S. Gribbs, the former Mayor of Detroit and a former resident. He was joined by several Detroit Lions players. Detroit Mayor Kwame Kilpatrick, accompanied by his family, and Michigan Attorney General Jennifer Granholm, a former Park resident, served as grand marshals in 2002.

Former Detroit Mayor Roman Gribbs in June Day parade

Linda Jamerson, the 2001 June Day chairperson, said, "Another June Day has come and gone. I have to admit I don't remember too much of what happened on Saturday, June 9, but I do remember seeing a lot of smiling faces. I met a gentleman who traveled 300 miles to be a part of our Rosedale Family reunion! I thought it was wonderful to know that no matter where your life leads you, the second Saturday in June you can come back home. I hope that everyone who attended walked away with rekindled love for the neighbors and this wonderful community."

That wonderful community was celebrated as the NRPCA received a grant from Detroit 300 for the "Rosedale Remembers" project to gather oral histories of current and former residents, artifacts, photos and other memorabilia to capture the history of the Park. The materials were featured in an exhibit, assembled by the Association and Park Players, at the Community House on June Day 2001 and periodically through December. The project was part of the yearlong celebration of the 300th anniversary of Detroit, founded in 1701.

Boy Scouts at campout, 1960
l-r: Fred Sumerton (Stahelin), Kenneth Chick (Glastonbury),
Ned Liddle (Westmoreland), Bruce Bieneman (Warwick)

As part of the "Rosedale Remembers" project, Bennett Young shared his experiences as a Boy Scout with Troop 123. "We would gather at the Community House, and we would hike from the clubhouse to Evergreen, up Evergreen, which turned into a gravel road, at maybe 7½ Mile, maybe Curtis, and we would walk up to 9 Mile ... That was Dun Scotus College in those days. On the southwest corner there must have been some 60 or 80 acres of woods and we would have campsites and we would go up there on Saturday morning, camp out overnight, and hike back on Sunday afternoon. The point is, from the time you got 6 blocks north of Six Mile, you were in the country. My parents moved into the Park around 1929 ... When my mother told her mother, my grandmother, that she was moving here, my grandmother was worried about her moving so far out into the boonies." Memory of the Park in 1930s-1940s for "Rosedale Remembers" Project

"When we moved to Detroit in 1952, we lived in an apartment at Forest and Second. In fact, it wasn't until 1959 that I really became aware of North Rosedale Park. We moved to Avon north of Seven Mile Road in 1958, and I drove on Outer Drive to Brightmoor Community Center on Burt Road daily, where I was program director. I knew that North Rosedale was all white and executives from corporations such as Edison and Excello lived there. I never expected to live there ... We were delighted to move into North Rosedale in 1978 in search of more space and soundproofing than we had on Avon. It's a move we loved. We glory in the fact that the neighborhood is integrated and is one where people live side by side, of all races, all occupations and work together for our local betterment." Maryann Mahaffey, Detroit City Council President, "Rosedale Remembers," 2001

Former City Council President
Maryann Mahaffey

Both the NRPCA and Park Players received awards from the Detroit 300 committee as heritage organizations for being in existence for 50 years or more.

The Association At Work

The Civic Association expanded its online reach by asking residents to provide their email addresses to receive information on events and programs in January 2000. The Association refreshed its site to make it more accessible and user friendly around the same time. The NRPCA also joined Facebook in 2009.

The Zoning and Restrictions Committee was reactivated in 2000 with the goal of developing long-term strategies to improve the appearance of the commercial strips in the area. The committee worked with other Association committees, Grandmont Rosedale Development Corporation and the business association to address concerns.

The committee adopted a new violation notice process in 2002 and provided copies of the ordinance violation notice in the *Tattler* for residents to use. Residents were encouraged to mail or place the notice in the violator's mailbox. If the violation was not addressed in 72 hours, they were to contact the 8th Precinct Environmental Task Force and then submit a copy of the notice to the committee if the violation was still not addressed. "This process does not eliminate the need for effective communication between neighbors. This process is a tool that can be utilized when communications break down between neighbors," said Anthony Abbott, NRPCA Board.

In keeping with its past focus on zoning restrictions, the Civic Association stated its opposition to a plan by a North Rosedale couple to open a tattoo and body piercing studio on Grand River in 2005. Although the City of Detroit had given conditional approval to the business, the NRPCA and Rosedale Park Improvement Association worked together to keep the business from opening and submitted a written request for appeal. However, the studio did open with no incidents.

The Zoning and Restrictions Committee was revived as the Code Enforcement Committee in 2009 to address zoning and code violations in the Park. The committee focused on educating residents on land use regulations; identifying problem areas; notifying homeowners of violations; and promoting enforcement by referring violations to the appropriate City department. Within six months, the team had identified 122 violations on properties, including debris, uncut grass, illegal dumping, unlicensed and commercial vehicles, poor property maintenance, buildings open to trespass, and improperly stored trash containers. By February 2010, 62 cases had been closed.

The Loss of a Park Leader

Taking a cue from government officials, the NRPCA held its first State of the Community Address in April 2002 as NRPCA President Linda Jamerson spoke to a packed house and touched on neighborhood safety, the Community House playground and leaders' efforts to reach out to teens causing problems in the Park. Board members gave a brief explanation of their areas of responsibility.

Linda Jamerson

The community address was a swan song of sorts for Jamerson, as she died suddenly in May 2002, marking the second time a NRPCA president had died in office. Her death left a hole in the hearts of many Park residents as evidenced by the many tributes in the June *Tattler*.

"For a true memorial to a very special and dear woman, step up and volunteer to make your community a better place. Volunteer for yourself and for Linda's memory. Both will be honored." Richard and Eleanor Dow

"You were my mentor in this process of living and serving in the new community that I have found my way to. But your shoes were too big and I can never fill them. Your vivaciousness, your energy, your beauty, inward and outward, your loving, caring, serving nature, your ideas, your intelligence, your challenge to all of us to do as well – I will sorely miss you." Caroline Landrum

Chuck Simms was appointed as president, and Anthony Abbott took over as vice president. At the end of his term, Simms said: "In retrospect, I have clearly learned two important lessons. First, I have more respect and appreciation for the hard work done by the presidents and board members who have come before me. Secondly, we desperately need more neighbors to get involved and play their part in the preservation of this great neighborhood. More importantly, I think we put forth the kind of effort that would have made Linda Jamerson proud."

The Association honored two hard-working Park residents, Tom and Chris Ridgway, with the Harry Gaither Award in September 2002 for outstanding service to the neighborhood. The Ridgways were involved in graffiti removal, planting and trimming trees and bushes, and beautification efforts around the Park. "Tom and Chris are the first to volunteer when a job needs doing. They do not wait to be asked and do not expect 'somebody else' to take care of the problems they see. They can be seen on the hottest summer days, weeding flower beds at the entrance to our community helping to make visitors' first impressions positive ones." Jan and Roger Halfacre

To keep up with the rising costs of maintenance of the Community House and park, the Association raised membership dues for 2003 to $50, a $10 increase. The next year, the organization increased membership dues for non-residents to $30, an increase of $5.

Tom and Christine Ridgway

Later in 2003, the Civic Association developed a financial plan to address financial shortfalls associated with June Day and the *Tattler*. Options included holding additional low-cost fundraisers to offset June Day expenses, reducing pages in the *Tattler*, delivering the publication to members only and eliminating home delivery. At the September membership meeting, Association members expressed concern about plans to reduce *Tattler* delivery and approved a motion for the board to meet with past presidents to discuss options. The resolution was to seek donations from members to specifically support the *Tattler*.

After some problems with distribution of the *Tattler* during the year, the Association decided to work with Park residents, including the youth, to distribute the publication, a practice used in the past.

As the Association was struggling financially, the organization received some good news as the Home and Garden Tour sold nearly 700 tickets and brought in $10,000 in revenue in fall 2003. Many called it the Park's best tour. "This tour exceeded all of our past efforts in several respects," said Duane Fueslein, tour co-chair. "First we were successful in making our tour known to the metropolitan area via a handsome poster, a second-to-none brochure, and what I believe to be North Rosedale Park's finest public relations piece in decades – a flattering article in the *Homestyle* section of *The Detroit News*." The tour featured six homes, two gardens, a landscape walk, and talk about one home's maintenance and restoration. Unique that year was the inclusion of classic cars, manufactured the year the home was constructed, parked in driveways.

The Association selected Dusing Security and Surveillance to provide patrol services in the Park in 2002. By December 2003, nearly 200 households had signed up, allowing the company to expand patrol services to 16 hours a day, seven days a week beginning in the new year. Yet, just months after the hours were expanded, the company had to reduce hours as residents failed to pay their subscriptions consistently.

No matter the decade, Park residents were concerned about crime. As neighbors got wind of crime reports, many bemoaned the acts with letters to the *Tattler* editor and pleaded with neighbors to subscribe to the patrol services, report crimes to the 8th Precinct and get to know their neighbors. "Subscribing to Dusing Security Service can't take the place of common sense ... of knowing your neighbors, turning on your porch light, locking your vehicle, or notifying authorities about non-functioning street lights ... If we had enough subscribers we would have someone patrolling their neighborhood 24 hours a day, 7 days a week. That's someone who's available to come and check out those things that could become police emergencies before they become police emergencies ... Dusing can't do more until we do more." Leslie Vaughn, Ashton Block Captain, December 2005

Unfortunately, sometimes the criminal acts were perpetrated by residents, which may have been the case with reports of vandalism at the Community House – destruction of lights and new trees, graffiti, and broken windows. The NRPCA board began researching surveillance systems to record activity around the clock.

More so, being a victim of crime can shake a person to the core. After being carjacked in her driveway at 5 p.m., Tamara Kamara, a former Association President, was ready to pick up and leave the Park in 2007. She had just turned off her car and opened the door, when she felt a gun to her head. The thief took her car, purse and the Harry Potter book she was reading.

"About 1 a.m. in the morning, I couldn't sleep. I wrote an email with the full description. I just sent it to everyone in the neighborhood in my contact list. At that point, I said that I was going to move because I didn't feel safe anymore."

The response to her email was unbelievable. "I got emails from perfect strangers offering to come and sit with me and pray for me. Then it dawned on me that I couldn't leave."

Her email made its way to a woman whose car was stolen from CVS. She contacted Kamara and provided the detective's number. The cases were connected. The police were ready to release the man with only a charge of joy riding. She went and identified the man, who eventually was sentenced to 14 years.

"It was all because of the neighborhood. Everyone really did wrap their arms around me. Some even offered to come to court with me."

Block Captains Hit the Streets

During the 2000s, the block captains were very active and organized a new event in June 2005 – Stoop Day. Neighbors were encouraged to sit on their front porch or steps or visit with each other, especially introducing themselves to neighbors they had never met and getting reacquainted with others.

The block captains also were the driving force behind re-establishing the North Rosedale Park volunteer CB Patrol program based on reports of neighborhood crime ticking up. The group planned to work in partnership with Dusing Security Services to patrol North Rosedale nights and weekends. The radio patrol began in spring 2009 with roughly 70 people signed up to participate.

Sunderland neighbors catch up on Stoop Day, 2006
l-r: Dot Clark, Linda Mahome, Mary Ratkowski and Tess Tchou

The monthly safety meeting program got its start the same year. The meetings, sponsored by the Association, included Detroit Police Department representatives and block captains and provided residents with safety tips for personal security and property protection.

As was the case over the years, it was always a challenge getting residents to join the NRPCA. In an effort to boost the number of members, the block captains went door-to-door in October 2004 talking to neighbors about the Association's purpose and activities and encouraging individuals to join the Association. The effort yielded some results as dues began rolling in even before membership letters were mailed.

Attracting members was a struggle, but so was finding individuals to run for the Association board. In 2005, only six individuals ran for board seats when normally a full slate would include twice the number of available seats. "Many of you have some great ideas, we need you to join the board, bring those ideas to the table, and put them into effect. We're not talking a lifelong commitment – just a few hours a month. Your participation is the only way the civic association can survive." Larry Davis, 2004 Association President

On the same subject, former Association President Anthony Abbott had a strong response to a resident with concerns about the quality of life in the Park. "North Rosedale Park is one of Detroit's gorgeous, precious gems, only needing the committed work of its neighbors to keep it sparkling. You want the board to address more of the issues that you wrote about, then give me the names of 11 dedicated, committed persons who will work and nominate for board seats each year. I currently have three. Do you know where I can find an additional 8? Are you willing to be #4? Give me a call and let me know."

Like with the Dutch Elm Disease, residents in the Park and across the region dealt with another invasive species: the emerald ash borer. General Motors donated $2500 to GRDC (thanks to Greg Hall) and another $2500 to The Greening of Detroit to address the trees in North Rosedale in 2005. The grant was seed money, and residents supported the pilot project to the tune of $70,000. The Association contributed $5000, Park Players $2000 and the Playground Fund donated $1500. Initially, 69 dead ash trees were removed and 99 new trees were planted. There were 29 dead trees on the Community

Volunteers learn about tree planting, 2005

House grounds alone. The tree project was led by the NRPCA beautification committee of Tom and Chris Ridgway, Greg Hall and Chris McEvoy.

The second phase focused on removing more dead ash trees scattered around the Park. With funds secured by GRDC, organizers were poised to plant another 184 new trees.

The Association got an unexpected gift of $2014 from Cooke School graduates in August 2006. The former students held a multi-year reunion for classes from 1970-1978 at the Community House. The reunion, two years in the making, drew more than 200 from all across the country including Alaska. Attendees were joined by Cooke teachers, Dorothy Lynch and Dorothy Koruga, and principal Dr. Leonard Zudick. The reunion committee, headed by Bernie Ball, agreed to donate remaining funds to the NRPCA, with an additional $800 donated to Cooke School. "Since our membership drives and our other fundraising events have been a little weak this year, this money is extremely appreciated," said Tom Ridgway, Cooke School Class of 1977 and NRPCA treasurer. He would know.

Later that year, the Association board voted unanimously to research historic designation for North Rosedale Park.

Park Hit by Housing Crisis

The mid-2000s were marked by financial turmoil across the country and in North Rosedale Park. The housing bubble collapse in 2006 and 2007 created a domino effect of falling property values, homeowners behind on their mortgages, and foreclosures of homes, all ending with a glut of vacant homes scattered across the Park. Community leaders estimated that 12 percent of the 1659 homes in the Park were vacant because of foreclosure, not including homes of residents at risk for foreclosure or those up for sale. The large number of vacant homes led to other problems, like an increase in squatters and theft of copper pipes, furnaces and water tanks. Residents also found their home values greatly reduced.

The housing crisis for Beverly Frederick represented both a low point and high point of her time in the Park. Frederick said it was painful "watching so many familiar faces walk away from their homes, due to the housing bubble and property tax foreclosures." She described it as devastating to the neighborhood.

Out of this uncertainty, the North Rosedale Park Civic Association created the Vacant Property Task Force. The magnitude of the crisis led to the task force being shifted to GRDC. Frederick described the task force as "hard working, dedicated volunteers, who were instrumental in changing the landscape of all five Grandmont Rosedale neighborhoods."

GRDC provided trained counselors to help those facing foreclosure or who had fallen behind on their mortgages. GRDC, in partnership with other organizations, sponsored a foreclosure prevention fair in November 2008, including representatives from the Wayne County Treasurer's Office, Assessors Office, and Mayor's Office, and foreclosure counselors, realtors, attorneys and short sale specialists. GRDC received a $9,600 grant from the Detroit Vacant Property Campaign in 2009 to board up homes, install security lights and provide for emergency lawn maintenance.

The Civic Association worked with local and state leaders to strengthen enforcement of City ordinances; gave input on developing legislation to address the problem; created a hotline for residents to report problems with property maintenance; and, later on, worked to promote the Grandmont Rosedale annual Neighborhood Open House. The *Tattler* carried articles on foreclosure prevention programs, reminding residents that they had options.

For some residents, like Marsha Bruhn, the situation was personal. "I was surrounded by houses that were in foreclosure and were blighted and run down," said Bruhn, who purchased and rehabbed three houses on her block between 2008 and 2012. "The whole idea was to get new homeowners, to stabilize the block and then in turn stabilize the neighborhood. I wanted to become part of the solution."

The housing crisis would continue into the next decade, with depressed housing prices bringing in a number of new neighbors who now could afford a home in the Park. The situation created some tension. In the past, while most buyers sought not just a home but a community, some newer residents were just looking for a house.

"Our community has a blueprint of being eclectic. Yet we still face a sense of entitlement, a feeling that only a certain type of person belongs here. A small number has those feelings," Frederick said. "However, we have some people that are jewels, people who are conscientious and understand that people are coming from a different place and they are to be embraced."

Frederick said the housing crisis also had a humbling effect. "There were a lot of people who were hurting, but they didn't want anyone to know. When you say North Rosedale Park, people are afraid of the stereotype associated with needing and receiving assistance."

Something positive occurred when North Rosedale Park and portions of Rosedale Park and Brightmoor were chosen as one of two pilot areas for the City's curbside recycling program in 2009. Residents received a recycling container, similar to the Courville container, to be placed at the curb every other week.

GRDC Continues Its Work

Grandmont Rosedale Development Corporation took residents, donors and funders on a neighborhood tour in May 2001. Participants learned about new playground equipment and improvements at several parks and schools; new businesses along Grand River; demolition of the old Shipley service station; home repairs for more than 40 residents; and the renovation and sale of more than 37 homes. "Almost all of our work is highly visible, things that people can see with their own eyes. Going out on a tour like this really brings home what a difference each person's contribution can make," said Tom Goddeeris, GRDC Executive Director.

The Grandmont Rosedale area got a new attraction as the Northwest Detroit Farmers' Market made its debut in July 2006. Located in the parking lot of Bushnell Congregational Church on Southfield Road, the market featured locally grown fresh fruits and vegetables, baked goods and bread and other prepared foods for sale and was sponsored and organized by GRDC. It was a small version

Shoppers look at produce at the Farmers' Market at Bushnell Congregational Church

of Eastern Market in northwest Detroit. During its first year, the market attracted more than 300 visitors each week.

While GRDC focused on business development and home renovations and repairs, residents took on the task of promoting the area. After attending an open house sponsored by the Stayers (Grandmont Rosedale Integrated Neighbors) in 1988, former Glastonbury resident Marsha Bruhn bought a house on Shaftsbury and wanted to re-establish the tour. "I thought that was such a successful event that I talked with some people about start-

Charles Pugh of FOX2 News interviews GRDC Executive Director Tom Goddeeris about open house, 2008

ing up the open house," Bruhn said. "We had a number of vacancies and wanted to attract homeowners."

The Grandmont Rosedale Neighborhood Open House, chaired by Bruhn and covered by TV and radio media, was held in May 2006, providing an opportunity for prospective home buyers to visit more than 60 homes that day. A joint effort by North Rosedale Park, Rosedale Park, Grandmont, Grandmont #1 and Minock Park, in collaboration with GRDC, the open house was held annually through 2018, attracting up to 400 attendees in some years and resulting in the sale of homes and new homeowners.

Alex Derdelakos expressed his enthusiasm for the event. "My wife and I were considering the neighborhood as a place to settle down, but it was the open house/neighborhood tour that really sold us. The event was a great way to learn about the community and its assets by seeing them in person with the guidance of its residents. We've been here for a year now and couldn't be happier with our decision to purchase a home in Rosedale Park."

GRDC got a new home when it purchased a vacant building at 19800 Grand River (formerly Plowden Martial Arts and

New headquarters for Grandmont Rosedale Development Corporation

Mural at Grandmont Rosedale Development Corporation headquarters

Michigan Secretary of State office before that). To cover the cost, GRDC launched a capital campaign to raise $300,000. The organization held its grand opening on May 22, 2008. Michigan artist Barney Judge was selected to create a wall mural for the new headquarters, paid for with a portion of the Cool Cities grant GRDC received on behalf of area neighborhoods.

The Spotlight Shines on Park Residents

Park Players celebrated its 50th anniversary in April 2003 with *Inside Out*, featuring a light-hearted musical revue written specifically to commemorate the milestone. The production incorporated songs from musicals performed by the troupe and included performances by four past Park Players presidents – Roger Loeb, Vicki Baldwin, George Evalt and Sally Goodman. "So happy birthday to my beloved Park Players! You've given not only to my family and so many other Park Players the opportunity to display talents onstage and off, but also have given the community so many wonderful moments of sheer entertainment. Thanks for the music, the comedy, the drama, the laughter, the tears, the emotion, the hard work, the friendships, and for my Park Family." Sally Evalt 2003

Young artists in the Park had a chance to show off their talents when the owners of Java in the Park sponsored the Young Artists Series in 2002. Darryl and Regina Horne, Rosedale Park residents, hosted a reception and displayed the artists' work for a month. "This series for young artists serves as another way to boost our connection to the community," said Regina Horne. The couple planned to feature a young artist's work every month. The artists

Young Artists Series featured Matthew and Ami Kamara

Young Artists Series also featured Sean and Jackie Wilke, here with Darryl Horne, Java in the Park owner

featured represented many Park families: Stark, Abe/Steigerwalt, Kamara, Smith, Cooper, Wilke, Garrett, Booth, Bland and Hejka. Just a month after their mother's death, the Jamerson children were the featured artists in June.

Joining the kids and Park Players in the spotlight were Park residents Jeffery and Cassandra Thomas, owners of Sweet Potato Sensations on Lahser Road in Old Redford. The Food Network's program, "The Best Of," hosted by Marc Silverstein, came to Detroit in April 2003 to do a feature on the company. The couple had operated the business since 1987 and produced a line of sweet potato products, including pies, cheesecakes, cakes, ice cream, cookies and cobblers. In 2009, the couple moved the business into its present location at 17337 Lahser Road.

North Rosedale Park resident Malcolm Collum could boast of doing his part to save a piece of American history. As a conservator with the Henry Ford Museum, Collum was involved with the acquisition and restoration of the bus that Rosa Parks rode on when she refused to give up her seat to a white man in December 1955. The Henry Ford Museum purchased and restored the bus, which is displayed at the museum.

Sweet Potato Sensations owners Cassandra and Jeffery Thomas with daughters, Jennifer and C.Espy

Children competing in Rosedale Soccer League

A keepsake from the last Woman's Club meeting, 2000

Players in the Rosedale-Grandmont Baseball League

Cooke STEM Academy students visit the Community House park

Neighbors enjoy each other during Shaftsbury block party

Former Cooke School students come together for a reunion, 2006

THE 2010S

Like previous decades, the 2010s were marked by highs and lows. The decade began with the signing of the Affordable Health Care Act (Obamacare); Wikileaks began spilling secrets and sensitive information; and Chilean miners were rescued after being trapped underground for 69 days.

The United States continued its fight against ISIS, killing Osama Bin Laden, the mastermind behind the 9/11 terrorist attacks. The country was shaken by news of the Boston Marathon bombing in 2013 and grappled with the Ebola virus.

Barack Obama began a second term in 2013, and the United States resumed diplomatic relations with Cuba in 2015. Donald Trump unexpectedly was elected president in 2016. Doctors saw the first signs of the coronavirus, though not yet identified, in late 2019.

The 2010s also were a time of instability and great change in Detroit. In 2013, the City of Detroit went through the largest municipal bankruptcy in the history of the United States, exiting bankruptcy 17 months later. After bankruptcy, a period of revitalization ensued with widespread investment in downtown Detroit, rising property values, and a renewed interest in Detroit.

In step with the growing cancel culture, the last vestige of former Park resident and Detroit Mayor Albert Cobo was removed as Cobo Center in downtown Detroit was renamed the TCF Center in August 2019. There weren't any protests against the move, as many considered Cobo to be a racist, an advocate of segregated housing and one who spearheaded urban renewal projects that razed black neighborhoods and businesses.

Attacking the Housing Crisis from All Sides

The housing and mortgage crisis that began in the late 2000s continued into this decade, which made the work of Grandmont Rosedale's Vacant Property Task Force even more important. The task force, working with the Grandmont Rosedale Development Corporation (GRDC), area realtors and the five neighborhood associations, was hard at work in 2009 and

2010: boarding up and painting the boards on 14 vacant homes; painting plywood boards on another 34 vacant homes; installing 70 solar security lights on vacant homes; and taking care of 110 lawns, some with extensive dumping problems.

As part of the effort to further address vacant homes across the five neighborhoods, GRDC received $1.4 million in financial support, including grants from the Kresge and Ford foundations, and a line of credit to finance renovation costs from Enterprise Detroit. Meanwhile, the organizers of the Grandmont Rosedale Neighborhood Open House were doing their part to promote the homes and began to see the fruit of their labor as individuals from metro Detroit and outside of Michigan purchased homes in the area. Leaders also credited positive news stories, GRDC's marketing program and housing affordability as other factors in influencing the moves. For those facing foreclosure, the Grandmont Rosedale communities worked together to provide information and resources.

Beverly Frederick cuts the lawn at a vacant home

Prospective buyers leave a home during the Grandmont Rosedale Open House

The Legacy Project Transforms the Community House

The year of 2011 represented the start of a transformation of North Rosedale's best asset – the Community House and surrounding park - as the Association embarked on a plan to make long overdue renovations. Led by NRPCA Vice President Jim Johnson and supported by a $34,000 grant from Kresge Foundation to U of D, the Association contracted with U of D's Detroit Collaborative Design Center (DCDC) to develop a conceptual design for the Community House. DCDC held a series of workshops and visioning sessions with neighborhood stakeholders to determine community vision and goals for the future of the Community House and grounds. DCDC's estimated cost for implementation of the resulting concept design was almost $2 million with another $500,000 for fundraising, program director and future capital maintenance.

Simultaneously, the Association, with legal assistance from Community Legal Resources, made plans to become a 501(c)(3) organization. Association members were asked to consider a number of revisions to the constitution and by-laws and to approve the Association's reinstatement of its articles of incorporation to be eligible for 501(c)(3) status by the IRS. A standing-room only crowd of members said yes to all the recommendations by a vote of 124 to 2 in May 2011. Johnson thanked John Burns, attorney and former Shaftsbury resident, for his invaluable advice and preparation of the application to the IRS.

The IRS approved the designation effective July 7, 2011, which allowed contributions to be tax deductible and for the Association to apply for philanthropic and government grants.

Even as plans were being formulated for major improvements to the Community House, work was still being done to the building. The roof was repaired; 16 security cameras were installed on the interior and exterior at a cost of $9,000; identification signs were repainted and updated and a new sign constructed outside the facility; and electrical repairs were completed.

As if there wasn't enough already going on, the nationally-known Project for Public Spaces organization (PPS) was working with GRDC to evaluate new locations for the Northwest Detroit Farmers' Market, as well as with the Association to improve its programming and management options. Based on PPS' recommendation, the Civic Association approved a request from GRDC to relocate the Farmers' Market to the NRPCA park grounds in February 2012, utilizing Kresge Foundation funds to expand and add lights to the south parking lot for that purpose. The market relocated to the parking lot in June 2014.

The capital campaign kicked into high gear in May 2012 at the home of Carol and Chris Allen with the first of many fundraising events. Attendees pledged $58,000. Combined with donations from Park Players and the Boy Scouts, the total raised was almost $70,000. Plans called for hiring a firm to develop a feasibility study and fundraising plan.

Based on a fundraising plan developed by the Association's consultant, Richner & Richner, the capital

A Redford Branch librarian reads to children at the Northwest Detroit Farmers' Market at the Community House

campaign was divided into phases, beginning with a phase one goal of $500,000. At this point, the campaign became officially known as The Legacy Project, chaired by Marsha Bruhn, with architect and former resident Don Scheible as NRPCA's owner's representative. Kresge Foundation funds enabled the NRPCA to hire Christie Peck for one year as a fundraising consultant to oversee all aspects of the capital campaign and work with the leadership committee and volunteers. Park resident Mary Davis was hired to assist her. The firm of Constantine George Pappas was contracted to prepare the master plan and design services for phase one.

A $500,000 project became $750,000 with the approval of a master plan for the Community House and grounds in March 2014.

Great news came with the announcement of a $50,000 donation to the capital campaign from former resident Jeff Adler in memory of his wife, Bonnie, in 2013. The Adlers had been active in Park Players, and Jeff shared comments about his role in *Guys and Dolls* at a reception at the Community House to thank him for his generous gift. With the additional gift of $100,000 from an anonymous donor the next year, a $194,000 grant from the City of Detroit, and donations from a mass appeal to current and former residents and friends, the campaign was off to a strong start.

The North Rosedale Park community celebrated as a groundbreaking ceremony in October 2014 marked the beginning of the transformation of the Community House with a 2,500-square-foot addition with large lobby, office and handicap-accessible restrooms. However, construction was delayed until spring while The Legacy Project's steering committee worked to reduce construction bids that came in higher than expected.

Construction on the new addition began in May 2015 while improvements to the interior of the building were underway. Thanks, in part, to a $24,000 grant from the Michigan Council for Arts and Cultural Affairs (MCACA), improvements included a fresh coat of paint in the

Association leaders, funders and dignitaries break ground for Community House addition
l-r: Gus Pappas (architect); Jim Johnson (leadership committee); Marsha Bruhn (capital campaign chair); Erma Leapheart-Gouch (NRPCA board); Don Scheible (owner's representative); Congressman John Conyers; Councilman James Tate; Laura Trudeau (Kresge Foundation); and *Free Press* columnist Rochelle Riley

Construction of the Community House addition

Marcia Closson at The Legacy Project Table Top Affair fundraiser

lobby, main hall and balcony; electrical work in the kitchen; and installation of LED lights and acoustical panels in the main hall.

The Legacy Project sponsored a successful Table Top Affair with the expertise of Park resident and designer Loretta Crenshaw, featuring designers with creative table arrangements; a raffle of two festive tables with china, silver and candlesticks; and a specialty boutique. The November 2015 event netted $25,000 to expand handicap accessibility at the Community House, and was the first event that included the new addition.

Excitement was in the air as Park residents gathered for a big celebration in December 2015 to commemorate the completion of the addition and the 75th anniversary of the Community House. The weekend began with the ribbon cutting for the addition followed by a party with music through the decades and concluded with a reverse raffle and silent auction. In all, the weekend events raised $20,681.

Success followed success. With three more Community Development Block Grant awards from the City, three more MCACA grants, foundation and corporate support, and individual donations, the NRPCA was able to replace the raised and flat roofs on the Community House, including installation of solar panels to reduce operating costs (2017); rebuild and expand the parking lot and circular driveway (2018); and create a concrete and exposed aggregate plaza adjacent to the new addition as an extension of the lobby and outdoor performance space (2018). Through the buy-a-brick campaign, 272 donors purchased engraved brick pavers installed in two areas of the plaza. Priorities changed over time, however, as projected costs increased, resulting in elimination for the present of elevator access to the second floor and an addition along the building's east end.

The Legacy Project's $76,000 grant from the Knight Foundation to fund two major art installations – a sculpture by esteemed Detroit artist and Rosedale Park resident Charles McGee on the plaza and a mosaic by noted muralist Hubert Massey at Cooke STEM Academy – brought public art to the Park. To raise the matching funds for the art installations, The Legacy Project conducted a crowdfunding campaign through Patronicity; sponsored a Park Players' production of *Sister Act*; held an art show and auction with the Detroit Fine Arts Breakfast Club; and sponsored a recital by Park resident and guitarist Peter Fletcher, all between March and September 2017. A fashion show – Living It, In the Park Fashion Extravaganza – in the fall promoted the brick campaign.

The Legacy Project art show and auction and fashion show, 2017

An audience of about 100 gathered on the plaza in September 2018 to dedicate the 24-foot metal sculpture by Charles McGee and to find their brick paver with family name or in memory of a loved one. The sculpture, entitled *Unity North*, is comprised of steel and aluminum, with a vibrant blue steel base with grey aluminum panels and 22 figures in white on each side. Installation of Massey's mural is anticipated for spring 2021. Inspiration for his design came from working with third- and fifth-grade students at Cooke and from a neighborhood focus group.

The things accomplished through The Legacy Project are a source of pride for Marsha Bruhn. It was one of her goals as Association President in 2011, along with Vice President Jim Johnson, to address the need for renovation of the Community House.

"It was such a gratifying experience to see the love that people have for this neighborhood and that I have for it. It has manifested itself in so many ways, and I had a hand in it," Bruhn said. "This was done with almost all volunteers – the planning, the fundraising, the overall management, the implementation. In 2012 if you had asked if all this was going to be

Donors look for their brick pavers on the newly constructed Community House plaza

Unity North sculpture and Community House addition and plaza

Hubert Massey's mural to be installed at Cooke STEM Academy

Artist Charles McGee, creator of the *Unity North* sculpture

Hubert Massey with a Cooke student showing his tile with design ideas for mural

done, I wouldn't have believed it. As I look back, I just want to cry."

Through grants, donations from more than 400 individuals and companies, and fundraisers over eight years, The Legacy Project raised more than $1.9 million. Recent projects include the 2019 renovation of the kitchen into a commercial kitchen through a $150,000 grant from the Michigan Economic Development Corporation (plus Legacy funds), and upgrades to the baseball and soccer fields with a Kresge Innovative Projects, Round 4 grant. A perimeter sidewalk and interior walking paths with Kresge funds are pending, along with a Detroit Water and Sewerage Department grant for plaza rain gardens and permeable paving. Four food entrepreneurs are utilizing the kitchen.

Bruhn said, "If we hadn't done what we've done, where would the Community House be? Many board members were opposed and asked, 'What sense does it make to invest in improvements when we are struggling to keep the lights on?' It is those improvements that have kept the lights on."

Financial Support Flows to North Rosedale Park

The Civic Association received two grants in early 2013 – $1,100 for vision screening during the annual Easter Egg Hunt and $900 for the Rosedale Grandmont Baseball League Opening Day. The League received a $5,000 grant from the Baseball Tomorrow Fund to cover a professional grant writer to assist in identifying additional funds for the renovation of four baseball fields at Stoepel Park #1 at Evergreen and W. Outer Drive. The baseball league also won $757 to purchase a storage pod at Stoepel Park during the Grandmont Rosedale SOUP dinner in October 2013.

Throughout the years, the North Rosedale playground received ample attention as committees worked to upgrade and refurbish equipment. The decade of the 2010s was no exception. During a storm in July 2010, a giant silver maple tree came crashing down on the playscape, destroying a good portion of it. The Association's insurance was expected to cover removing the tree and repairing the playscape.

More recently, the playground committee raised funds to provide a wheel-

Playground at Community House with improvements for children with disabilities

chair-accessible playground surface along with new play equipment accessible to sensory sensitive children and others with disabilities, for an inclusive playing experience. As part of its commitment to the Grandmont Rosedale neighborhoods, TCF Bank contributed $45,000 to the $75,000 raised in total. Improvements were completed in March 2020, just before the COVID-19 shutdown.

Association Still Hard at Work, Though Struggling

The election of the 2010 NRPCA board ushered in a board dominated by women. Of the 15 members, 13 were women.

Guess who's coming to … lunch? Mayor Dave Bing and his wife, Yvette, were invited to join the North Rosedale Park Civic Association's Garden Tour luncheon in July 2010.

The North Rosedale Park community came out to celebrate Lavonne Thomas later that year as she retired after more than 19 years of dedicated service as building manager for the Civic Association and all-around volunteer.

Even with the success of the capital campaign, the Civic Association grappled with budget shortfalls for a number of years. For some it seemed that the fundraising efforts of the capital campaign were cutting into income for the Association. However, a financial review revealed that financial shortfalls were occurring in the 2000s as well, before the start of the campaign. The Association voted to raise membership dues for 2015 to $75 per household to offset higher operating expenses.

"On a very serious note, the NRPCA is really short on cash. The Capital Campaign currently does not have an operations component. That means money for lights, heat and maintenance of the Community House and the *Tattler* and our beloved but non NRPCA fundraising activities … come out of your membership dues, our fundraisers, and our Community House rentals. We have a shortfall every year; our emergency fund is depleting. The good news is that we have an action plan, but we really need your help," said NRPCA President Susan Steigerwalt, April 2015.

As a visible example of the severity of the Association's finances, Park residents received a *Rosedale Tattler* with only four pages and no color in September 2015. Steigerwalt issued an urgent plea: "This four-page *Tattler* is an illustration of what the future of the *Tattler* may be if the NRPCA does not quickly acquire additional financial support … There is no community without neighbors, so neighbors, we are asking for your help." The good news: NRPCA ended the year in the black.

In another cost-cutting move, the *Tattler* went from a monthly publication to bi-monthly publication in November 2019.

Although The Legacy Project was a major effort of the NRPCA, the organization continued to make improvements and create programs and activities for its members. The *eBlast* newsletter for North Rosedale Park was launched in April 2013 to supplement the printed *Rosedale Tattler*.

Thanks to a $5000 grant from Healthy Environments Partnership (HEP) with the University of Michigan, a certified walking group was formed in 2012. Participants took part in health screenings to measure the benefit of walking and received t-shirts, whistles, mace, reflective vests and other items as incentives.

"We found that the walking group was beneficial to so many, including people who lost weight and were able to get off medication," said Gloria Goodwine, who coordinated the group. "They gained their health back." The Association received an additional $2000 grant in 2015 to continue the program.

Goodwine filled out the remaining months of a grant shared jointly by NRPCA and GRDC to fund two Public Allies to work on developing programming in 2014, then continued with program director activities at the end of the grant. Other programming included Book Club in the Park, Aikido, Zumba and Yoga classes, along with a summer dance camp for children in 2015. The offerings expanded to include Pilates, Hustle and ballroom dancing classes, decorating, sewing and a healthy eating class.

Alongside the programs offered, the Association created two new groups – Grandmont Rosedale Young Professionals for young adults and the Teen Council for high school students, led by board member Kim Dorsey along with other board members and volunteers. In November 2019, the NRPCA launched a workshop series with classes ranging from bicycle maintenance to security systems to soap making.

Programs offered at the Community House included Pilates and martial arts

North Rosedale Park: Still the Home of Leaders

Resident Sherry Gay-Dagnogo, a former Detroit Public School teacher and Educational Performance Director for United Way of Southeastern Michigan, was interviewed by Dan Rather for his documentary, *A National Disgrace*, which aired in May 2011. Gay-Dagnogo said, "While the documentary did not showcase the pockets of excellence in our educational system, it highlights some inconvenient truths we must be willing to assess where we are, and put our agenda aside to embrace Innovation with positive change."

Sherry Gay-Dagnogo appeared in Dan Rather's documentary, *A National Disgrace*, 2011

In addition, the Civic Association established a community partnership with Cooke School to assess the school's needs in 2013. As a part of that effort, the group planned to recruit volunteers, including some of the Park's leaders, to assist with tutoring and mentoring, and organize healthy cooking lessons and fitness programs.

NRPCA Vice President Richard Castillo passed suddenly in July 2016 while diving in Lake Huron. His life and contributions to North Rosedale Park were celebrated during a memorial service at the Community House in October 2016. "We are a great community because of people like Richard and because of people like you. I appreciate him for all he did and for who he was and all of you for the kindness, thoughtfulness and selfless contributions made on behalf of our NRPCA home." Erma Leaphart-Gouch, Civic Association President 2016

Richard Castillo

Park Players to Return?

Park Players recognized its 60th anniversary with a special celebration in June 2013 that included a meal followed by performances featuring songs from productions over the years. Since its creation in 1953, the theater troupe had performed roughly 140 shows.

After 64 years as the theater troupe for North Rosedale Park, Park Players moved to the Redford Theatre in 2018. There were some mixed feelings and tensions surrounding the move. On the one hand, the Association board was looking for ways to shore up its finances and establish rental fees based on market rates. On the other hand, Park Players felt the rental costs for the Community House were too high and would force the troupe to charge unreasonable ticket prices. After a successful weekend at the Redford Theatre with the play, *Shrek*, the troupe thought the theatre was ideal and would draw more patrons.

Park Players signed a three-year contract with the Redford Theatre but left after the second year. "They also wanted to increase our fees, and it was hard to attract people from the Park, just a mile away, and those from the other side of Telegraph," said Archie Lynch, Park Players President. "It seems people like to see old movies but not live theatre."

All is not lost as Park Players is looking to return to the Park. A troupe called the Scarsdale Players performed *A Raisin in the Sun* at the Community House in 2019 utilizing Park Players members.

"We were hoping to do something this year for the NRPCA and start getting the theatre back in North Rosedale Park. We always like being at the Community House," Lynch said. Park Players has been in conversation with the Civic Association, but hasn't yet signed a contract.

The Special Assessment District That Was

GRDC launched several efforts to address neighborhood safety during the decade. One was a new community crime alert website in 2010, allowing residents to sign up for crime alerts, and a separate security blog for residents to discuss community security topics. The Neighborhood Safety Meetings, organized by GRDC, were another means of providing information on crime and safety matters and served as a connection between Grandmont Rosedale residents and the Detroit Police Department.

Its most ambitious effort was taking the lead in 2011 in creating a Special Assessment District (SAD) ordinance for Detroit with the goal of getting property owners' approval for the district in North Rosedale, Rosedale Park, Grandmont, Grandmont #1 and Minock Park. Karen Johnson Moore was tapped to lead the effort with assistance from GRDC staff, area residents and a team of interns. What started as a one-year project for Moore morphed into five years.

First, there was the matter of lobbying State legislators to lower the law's population requirement from 750,000 to 600,000 residents as Detroit's population dropped. Then the matter had to be approved by the Detroit City Council and Emergency Manager Kevyn Orr, which eventually gave their blessing. To establish the district, 51 percent of homeowners had to agree to pay additional taxes to cover security and snow removal – something that North Rosedale residents wanted but often were not willing to pay. Under the SAD, property owners would pay for the services as expenses were spread over the five areas, reducing the cost to individual homeowners.

However, by the time GRDC was ready to gather the necessary signatures of roughly 5600 households, the opposition came out and launched the Say No to SAD campaign.

"There were a handful of people who got riled up and didn't understand the value of GRDC," Moore said. "This is something that the community wanted and we're just moving forward with it."

Moore said that the opposition didn't want to pay higher taxes for the services and had a distrust or misconception of GRDC. "There were a lot of people who didn't trust GRDC or who didn't know about GRDC. There was the idea that GRDC wanted to make money off of it." She also believes that many NRPCA and GRDC board members were not vocal enough about the merits of SAD.

"It was probably the most ambitious thing we ever tried to do," said Tom Goddeeris, GRDC Executive Director at the time. "I think that all five neighborhoods initially agreed to support the effort but not each group was equally committed to the idea. It was too high of a bar."

As both Goddeeris and Moore look back, both say they would have done things differently. "If I were to go back in time, I would have done it neighborhood by neighborhood," Goddeeris said. "It took awhile for the legislation to pass and then there were so many residents behind in their taxes. So there was opposition to a tax increase."

For Moore, the effort needed a comprehensive public relations campaign to inform people about GRDC and to promote the advantages of SAD. "We did all of this work, and we were left hanging in the wind." It wasn't all for naught, however, as Palmer Woods, Sherwood Forest and Detroit Golf Club communities approved a Special Assessment District in 2016.

A Mixed Bag

There was sad news in 2011 when Boy Scout Troop 123 announced it was dissolving because of declining membership. As a parting gift to the North Rosedale Park Civic Association, the troop donated $4,209 in appreciation for the organization's sponsorship of the troop over the years. Roughly six years later, the leaders of Boy Scout Troop 123 announced plans to restart the troop, starting on June Day with an open house and scouting exhibit.

Mayor Duggan explains plan to install LED lights in North Rosedale Park, 2014

Josh White Jr. came home to give a full concert performing blues, folk, spiritual and jazz at the Community House in April 2012. He returned for another concert in May 2015.

Once again, North Rosedale could boast of being chosen for a pilot program by the City of Detroit. It was curbside recycling back in 2009. In 2014, it was LED streetlights. Mayor Mike Duggan and the Public Lighting Authority announced at a February meeting at the Community House that North Rosedale and part of Rosedale Park would get new LED streetlights under an accelerated program. Crews completed installation on residential streets and major thoroughfares later that year.

Children stock the new Little Free Library at the Community House

The Little Free Library (LFL) made its Detroit debut, right here in North Rosedale Park in fall 2014. The non-profit organization promotes community book exchanges and a love of reading. LFL Executive Director Todd Bol donated the library to the Park hoping media coverage would spur others in Detroit to purchase and install one. The library was installed near the park playground and is stocked regularly with children's and adult books.

For June Day 2016, North Rosedale Park welcomed local and state elected officials as grand marshals. They included

Mayor Mike Duggan, State Senator David Knezek and Wayne County Commissioner Burton Leland, along with Councilman James Tate and State Representative Sherry Gay-Dagnogo, both Park residents.

Finalists in NRPCA Reverse Raffle fundraiser, 2018

Park residents sample entries in chili cook-off contest

New lobby at the Community House

NRPCA receives $150,000 from State of Michigan for commercial kitchen, 2018
Front row, l-r: Ian Watts (North Rosedale), Bill Frey (NRPCA President), State Rep. Sherry Gay-Dagnogo, Sherita Smith (GRDC Executive Director), State Senator David Knezek, Tess Tchou (Kitchen Committee) and Marsha Bruhn (The Legacy Project chair)
Back row: Alex Derdelakos (Rosedale Park) and Theresa Glenn (NRPCA director)

Home Sweet Home

Over the decades, North Rosedale Park has hosted a multitude of events and programs, some of which have come, gone and returned years later. That list includes the Ice Carnival, Park Fair, summer recreation program, Mother's Day and Christmas breakfasts, baseball, basketball and soccer leagues, men's and women's bowling leagues, ice skating and hockey, CB patrol, Boy and Girl Scouts, Easter Egg Hunt, Halloween parties, JA dances, luncheons for seniors, nursing scholarships, and the list goes on.

Among those activities, June Day and Steak Roast have stood the test of time and become cherished traditions that residents, both current and former, embrace. Each year, without fail, June Day and Steak Roast bring neighbors and friends together to celebrate what makes North Rosedale Park so special.

While the events and programs are truly drawing cards, most would agree it is the people of North Rosedale who make the neighborhood what it is. The common theme throughout the decades, from the pioneers until now, is the fond

l-r: Roland Breech and Cheryl Buswell Robinson handle cooking duties at Steak Roast; in the background are Bob Weed and Hubert Sawyers

memories that many, if not most, have of life in North Rosedale Park. Those memories are what compelled Josh White III to organize several reunions of fellow Benedictine students and Park residents since 2013. "Back in 2010 when I joined Facebook, I ended up reconnecting with 90 percent of the people that I went to high school

Josh White III and friends gather for a reunion

with. I said 'we need to get together' and so the group did." The first time about 30 showed up for a softball game and 75 for the reunion. The reunion was a way to reconnect and reminisce about good times, White said.

For Amy Vargo Oaks, moving back to North Rosedale Park has had its ups and downs. After taking care of her parents, who have passed, she stayed. "The thing that hasn't changed is the people that live here. We are cohabiting and you care for each other. There's been crime, break-ins and that has come in waves, but in spite of that, people look out for each other."

She has been involved in several activities including making June Day signs and recruited her neighbors to help. "A lot of people that I grew up with are still on this block," Oaks said. "It's one of the things that makes this area special. You have to jump in and do and be a part of the community."

Elaine Lewis Hendrix has no regrets about living in North Rosedale Park, even today. "It was important to raise our kids in an integrated community, and they got that here in Rosedale Park. The fact that my kids enjoyed their time in Rosedale Park is very important to me." Hendrix believes that their experience with the baseball league is one of the reasons that her children, Erin and Stephen, have such fond memories. She recalled a time when her daughter, Erin, tried out for a part with Park Players at age 12 because she was confident. "When kids grow up with confidence and comfortability like they received here in our community, it makes them leaders. It has roots and it stays with these kids."

Mary Lou Miller, who has lived in the Park for 78 years, has a lifetime of memories. "The wonderful thing about growing up in North Rosedale Park is we weren't just family-oriented, but community-oriented. We prided ourselves on knowing just about everyone and doing lots of things here," said Miller. "I have always loved Detroit. I would never think of moving to the suburbs."

This is the North Rosedale Park envisioned by Harry St. John in his series of 14 articles on the history of the neighborhood that ran in the *Tattler* from October 1934 until March 1937. Noting challenges facing the Association in the March 1937 *Tattler*, St. John wrote, "It is apparent that the future of the association and of the community as we have known it, depends upon the successful outcome of the present efforts to solve these problems ... There is every reason to hope that Rosedale Park's present obstacles can be surmounted, as they have in the past, but it ... requires the whole hearted efforts of every resident of Rosedale who values its unique community life and the opportunities which it affords to him and his family. If enough people value it sufficiently there need be no doubt as to the outcome."

After one hundred years of history filled with triumphs and challenges, the vast majority of Park residents and friends would agree that the outcome has been good.

Noted North Rosedale Park Residents

Chris Allen, Health Care Executive and Authority Health CEO, **Bretton Drive**

John Amberger, Southeast Michigan Council of Governments (SEMCOG) Executive Director, **16514 Edinborough**

Wendell Anthony, Detroit NAACP President and Fellowship Chapel Pastor, **Warwick**

Janeé Ayers, Detroit City Council, **Ashton**

Donald Ball, *Detroit News* Reporter, **15892 Rosemont**

Mary Ball, International Institute Executive Director, **15892 Rosemont**

Leland Bassett, CEO Bassett & Bassett Inc., **18644 Gainsborough**

Tina Bassett, President of Bassett & Bassett Inc., **18644 Gainsborough**

Christine Beatty, Chief of Staff for Mayor Kwame Kilpatrick, **16610 Westmoreland**

Bob Berg, Press Secretary for Mayor Coleman Young, **16800 Glastonbury**

Mary Jane Bigler, Michigan Watercolor Society Founder, **16708 Rosemont**

Patricia Boyle, Michigan Supreme Court Judge, **15925 Warwick**

Terrance Boyle, Wayne County Circuit Court Judge, **15925 Warwick**

Marsha Bruhn, City of Detroit City Planning Commission Director, **Shaftsbury**

John Burns, Attorney for 1975 Blockbusting/Solicitation Lawsuit, **16715 Shaftsbury**

Keith Butler, Detroit City Council Member and Bishop of Word of Faith International Christian Center, **19160 Bretton Drive**

Bartlett Lee Clark, Commander of the Nuclear Submarine USS Omaha, **Sunderland**

Elbernita "Twinkie" Clark, Member of Gospel Group Clark Sisters, **15919 Avon**

Albert E. Cobo, Detroit Mayor 1950-1957, **16873 Huntington**

Loretta Crenshaw, Decorator, Crenshaw & Associates, **Plainview**

Matt Cullen, Bedrock CEO and Detroit Riverfront Conservancy Chair, **15604 Glastonbury**

Sherry Gay-Dagnogo, Michigan House of Representatives, 8th District, **Glastonbury**

Frankie Darcell, Radio Personality, **18863 Gainsborough**

Gershwin Drain, U.S. District Court Judge, **Westmoreland**

Bobby Ferguson, Demolition Company Owner and Kwame Kilpatrick Associate, **Bretton Drive**

Peter Fletcher, Classical Guitarist, **Lancashire**

John "Frenchy" Fuqua, NFL Player with N.Y. Giants and Pittsburgh Steelers 1969-78, **16740 Sunderland**

Hilary Golston, Fox 2 Reporter and Anchor, **W. Outer Drive**

Amanda (Amy) Good, Alternatives for Girls CEO, **Rosemont**

Jennifer Granholm, Michigan Governor 2003-2011, **18707 Gainsborough**

Roman S. Gribbs, Detroit Mayor 1970-1974, **16515 Edinborough**

Martha Griffiths, Michigan Lt. Governor under James Blanchard 1983-1991, **16603 Warwick**

Thomas Hearns (The Hitman), Professional Boxer, **19300 Bretton Drive**

Elaine J. Hendrix, Detroit Tigers Vice President, **Bretton Drive**

Freman Hendrix, Deputy Mayor under Mayor Dennis Archer, **Bretton Drive**

Adrienne Hinnant-Johnson, 36th District Court Judge, **Westmoreland**

Sarah Hulett, Michigan Radio Senior Editor, **Gainsborough**

Wendy Jackson, Managing Director for the Detroit Program for Kresge Foundation, **Huntington**

Harold Johns, Park Motor Sales Owner, **15830 Warwick**

Alex Johnson, Major League Baseball Player, **18425 Bretton Drive**

Robert Jones, Musician & WDET Host of "Blues from the Lowlands," **18645 Gainsborough**

Kwame Kenyatta, Detroit City Council 2006-2013, **18534 Bretton Drive**

Richard Kughn, Lionel Trains Owner & Taubman Centers Executive, **18944 Bretton Drive**

James E. Lacey, Wayne County Probate Court Judge 1978-2007, **16735 Ashton**

Dr. Richard Levinson, City of Detroit Public Health Director, **18877 Bretton Drive**

Maryann Mahaffey, Detroit City Council Member and President 1974-1998, **19405 Bretton Drive**

Latrice McClendon, TCF Bank Vice President of Corporate Community Relations, **Rosemont**

Dr. Florian Muske, Detroit Red Wings Team Dentist 1949-1983, **19544 Bretton Drive**

Larry Nevers, Detroit Police Officer Involved in Malice Green Case, **19327 Bretton Drive**

Ted Nugent (Motor City Madman), Singer, Songwriter and Political Activist, **15963 Warwick**

L. Brooks Patterson, Oakland County Executive 1993-2019, **16751 Glastonbury**

David A. Perkins, Wayne County Probate Court Judge, **Rosemont**

Suren Pilafian, Architect and Industrial Designer, **Florence**

Kevin Porter, Professional Basketball Player with Detroit Pistons, **19260 Bretton Drive**

Mel Ravitz, Detroit City Council Member and President 1961-1973, 1981-1997, **16160 Warwick**

June Ridgway Roselle, Detroit Chief Assessor & Civic Center Director, **16615 Ashton**

Rollo Romig, Journalist and Critic, **18690 Gainsborough**

Jimmy Settles, UAW Vice President, **18817 Bretton Drive**

Leon Spinks, Professional Boxer, **19300 Bretton Drive**

Frank Stella, F.D. Stella Products Company Founder and CEO, **19180 Gainsborough**

Emanuel Steward (Manny), Professional Boxer and Trainer, **19260 Bretton Drive**

Anthony Szymanski, Wayne County Probate Court Judge, **15766 Glastonbury**

James Tate, Detroit City Council Member 2009-Present, **Scarsdale**

Heather Ann Thompson, Historian and Pulitzer Prize-Winning Author, **Bretton Drive**

Saskia Thompson, Detroit Land Bank Authority Director, **Bretton Drive**

Tyrone Tillery, Detroit NAACP Executive Secretary, **18131 Keeler**

Reginald Turner, Attorney and American Bar Association President-Elect, **18450 Bretton Drive**

Jerome Vaughn, WDET News Director, **Ashton**

George Ward, Wayne County Chief Assistant Prosecutor 1986-2000, **18853 Bretton Drive**

Josh White Jr., Musician and Actor, **19191 Lancashire**

Chuck Wilbur, WDET News Director, **16753 Warwick**

Steve Wilke, Journalist and Hour Detroit Magazine Editor, **Edinborough**

North Rosedale Park Civic Association Presidents

From 1923-1935, officers served from October-September for two terms.

Jacob G. Judson, 1923-1925
Clarence L. Weaver, 1925-1927
Harry St. John, 1927-1929
William H. Hudson, 1929-1931
Jack Lillie, 1931-1933
Arthur Nicklet, 1933-1935

In 1935, the Association changed its fiscal year to end in December.

Arthur Siebert, 1936-1937
Herbert Wilbraham, 1938-1939
Lewis Judson, 1940-1941
Leland Place, 1942-1943
Dr. Andrew Pringle, 1944-1945
Marshall Allen, 1946-1947
Herbert Schoenberg, 1948-1949

Association presidents served for two years prior to 1950.

Lacey Laughlin, 1950
Walter Bieneman, 1951
Edwin Husen, 1952
Donald Kaump, 1953
Holland D. Weir, 1954
Milton Drake, 1955
David Batey, 1956
William Wickham, 1957
Albert Finly, 1958
Vincent Keyes, 1959
Dr. Philip Gelbach, 1960
Robert Rutherford, 1961
DeWitt Severance, 1962 (died in office in August)
William Stockwell, 1962-1963
   (served for remainder of term)
Kenneth Wigle, 1964
Robert Sturwold, 1965
George Rice, 1966
L. David McCabe, 1967
George Harding, 1968
August Blomquist, 1969
Edward Hoisington, 1970
Lawrence O'Connor, 1971
Charles Allegrina, 1972
Fred O'Dras, 1973
James Wetzel, 1974
George Marshall, 1975

Don Myers, 1976
Stuart Smith, 1977
J. William Sheppard, 1978
Beth Burns, 1979 (first female president)
George Ward, 1980
William Baird, 1981
Sharon Lippe, 1982 (second female president)
Arnold Rzepecki, 1983
Mike Donahue, 1984
Paul Bourlier, 1985
Clay Blaesser, 1986
Don Scheible, 1987
Sally Evalt, 1988
Bill Campbell, 1989
Christine Davis, 1990
Delphine Tupper, 1991
   (first African-American president)
Chris Allen, 1992
   (first African-American male president)
Freman Hendrix, 1993
Jim Johnson, 1994
Bill Frey, 1995
Marcia Closson, 1996
Becky Blaesser, 1997
Kris Dighe, 1998
Rick Garrett, 1999
Maurice Dewey, 2000
Richard Dow, 2001
Linda Jamerson, 2002 (died in office in May)
Chuck Simms, 2002 (served for remainder of term)
Anthony Abbott, 2003
Larry Davis, 2004
Duane Fueslein, 2005
Tamara Kamara, 2006
Dwayne Walker, 2007
Carla Thomas, 2008
Wendy Lewis Jackson, 2009
Lynn Garrett, 2010
Marsha Bruhn, 2011
Jim Johnson, 2012
Cheryl Buswell Robinson, 2013
Hubert Sawyers, 2014
Dr. Susan Steigerwalt, 2015
Erma Leapheart-Gouch, 2016
Tamara Kamara, 2017
Bill Frey, 2018-2019
Wendy Lewis Jackson, 2020

NORTH ROSEDALE PARK HIGHLIGHTS

Rosedale Park Woman's Club

Since its incorporation in 1923 until its 75th anniversary celebration in 1999, the Woman's Club was an energetic force in building and maintaining the social fabric of North Rosedale Park. It was organized to strengthen the bond of neighborliness. Begun as a small sewing circle, with women taking linens to hem or socks to darn in members' homes, the afternoons getting acquainted led to a highly organized club that met monthly at the Community House and grew to include 28 committees and 538 members by its 50th anniversary in 1973. It was one of the oldest established and largest women's organizations in Detroit.

Members were quite formal, wearing hats and gloves to meetings and enjoying the beautiful tea service. President Shirley O'Donnell tells the story of her invitation to attend the Woman's Club friendship luncheon, arriving in her best white suit with red accessories, only to be told by an elderly member, "I know you are a foreigner in this country, but we have a rule about white suits; you can only wear them after Memorial Day and before Labor Day. You'll know next time."

In spite of the formality, the women hosted numerous charitable works – Christmas parties for less fortunate children; dress drives for needy girls; donating clothing and personal items for abused women; and financial assistance for Detroit City College, U of M and Wayne State University students. Activities expanded dramatically during World War II as they focused on aiding the war efforts by raising funds, preparing convalescent kits, collecting clothing, and supplying food and service for members of the armed forces at the downtown Detroit USO Canteen.

As times changed, so did the organization by recognizing members by their names and not their husbands, dropping hats and gloves, and becoming more racially diverse. In the years leading up to its 75th anniversary in 1999, membership had dropped as more women worked and lifestyles changed. The Club dissolved in 2000, but the memories endure of an association that created a strong circle of friends, who participated in a wide variety of worthwhile activities that greatly enriched their years in North Rosedale Park.

June Day

It is a testament to the early settlers of North Rosedale Park, and to those who came after, that a tradition begun in 1930 endures to this day. Even the parade route set at that time – Bretton to Outer Drive and return – has endured. Imagine hundreds and hundreds of children and adults gathering to enjoy a day full of fun, beginning with a parade featuring bands, decorated floats and bikes, games and races, plus prizes for best floats, marchers, race winners, clowns and impersonators. For many years, the day lasted from noon until midnight, with the 1957 June Day ending with a dance for 320 young people.

A fixture at June Day was bandmaster Larry Vroom, who led the parade for 28 consecutive years from 1935 to 1962. He served as music and band instructor at Cooke School for many years. Events often followed the times. The June 9, 1945 celebration featured prizes for floats in military and patriotic categories. Junior Activities Committee programming included penny scramble, peanut race, pole climbing, tug-of-war, and relays, with categories for Cub, Girl and Boy Scouts and Camp Fire Girls.

"Womanpower" was the word in the Tattler for June Day 1973 as almost 70 women registered participants, judged contestants, and manned the ticket booth and food tent. Men oversaw the midway – dunk tank, crazy ball, jarco, spindle game, hula hoop, lollipop tree and fishing pond. A chicken dinner by "Col. Sanders" was served behind the Community House accompanied by the Franklin Village Brass Band.

June Day grand marshals have ranged from Detroit mayors to radio and TV personalities to prominent Park residents, such as Mayor Roman Gribbs and Michigan Attorney General (and later Governor) Jennifer Granholm. Grand marshals in recent years have included Beth Burns, the first female president of the NRPCA, and past presidents.

The parade, track and field events, costumes and floats, midway, prizes, and a picnic supper, followed by a concert or movie (sometimes both) have made June Day an event to look forward to, and to remember.

Park Players

North Rosedale Park's popular theatre group, Park Players, can trace its beginning to the entertainment committee of the Civic Association, which put on its first production, a minstrel show in May 1947. In 1953, the Civic Association proposed a new theatrical group and invited Park residents to join. Park Players, an official NRPCA organization, established its own officers and board. The troupe began by performing one-act plays in December 1953. Admission was $1. The group progressed to a musical each spring and a comedy or drama in the fall. Periodically, it would put on a summer production or children's show. The group evolved to near professional status and became one of the oldest community theatre groups in the area.

Musical productions have included *Oklahoma, Pajama Game, Guys and Dolls*, and *Dreamgirls*, the last such a success that additional play dates had to be added to meet demand. Fall plays have included *The Prime of Miss Jean Brodie* and Agatha Christie's *A Murder is Announced.*

Ingrid Small, a Park resident, commented on her involvement with Park Players. "I want to express my deepest appreciation to the Park Players ... I have learned so much from them while performing ... I want everyone to know you may have talent but to have a place like our Community House where you can develop and show it has made all the difference in my life." Small was graduating from Cass Tech at the time and going on to Oakland University on a full theatre scholarship. (June 1994 *Tattler*)

As times changed, so did the group. The original requirement that Park Players members had to be members of the Civic Association and live in North Rosedale Park was changed to allow membership to anyone. Once a committee of the Association, it severed its ties to the NRPCA on September 21, 1989. A dramatic change occurred when Park Players left its home of 65 years at the Community House in spring 2018 and moved to the Redford Theatre where the larger theatre could accommodate a broader audience. That partnership ended in 2019. Longtime fans of the theatre group were elated when current and former Players, calling themselves the Scarsdale Players, returned to the Community House in fall 2019 for *A Raisin in the Sun* by Lorraine Hansberry. *A Christmas Carol* planned for November 2020 by Park Players was cancelled, like everything else, because of the pandemic.

Home & Garden Tour

A tradition since the 1960s, the Home & Garden Tour has been a way to show off the historic homes and gardens of North Rosedale Park and promote the neighborhood socially, economically and culturally as a community of choice. North Rosedale Park joins historic Detroit neighborhoods, such as Indian Village and Boston Edison, in promoting the best of city living.

The tours were sponsored by the Woman's Club until 1989, when the Association organized the tour for the first time. Names changed over the years: Autumn Open House Tour in 1967, Rosedale Renaissance Christmas Walk in 1974, Glow of Christmas in 1980, Rosedale at Twilight in 1982, House and Garden Walk in 1987, Green Garden Tour in 2009, and Home and Garden Tour in 2013.

Like June Day, a successful event requires long-term planning and the involvement of many volunteers. Efforts are made each year to select homes reflective of the diversity of the neighborhood, both in the style of the homes and the residents of the community. Gardens, too, have reflected a variety of styles ranging from the simple homeowner garden-landscape to those of the master gardener.

The Home and Garden Tour committee's slate is full as it selects the homes and gardens, recruits and trains docents, assists homeowners with preparing and staging their homes, and provides lunch on the day of the tour. In later years, the day ended with an afterglow on the front lawn of the Community House where homeowners and volunteers were celebrated for their contributions to the event.

Special features have included a bazaar with handmade items by Club members, dollhouse display, photographic exhibition, scavenger hunt, and a classic car at each home from the year the home was constructed. The 2010 tour was attended by Mayor Dave Bing and featured "the Red House," so called because of its romantic 1920s design woven around the theme of glitz, glamour, champagne and red. Proceeds in earlier years benefited the Geriatrics Fund of the Woman's Club, and, more recently, upkeep of the Community House and park.

Finding residents willing to open their homes for tours became increasingly difficult in recent years, requiring the committee to limit the tour to only gardens one year and forgoing a tour altogether for a few years. One is planned, however, for August 2021 in conjunction with the North Rosedale Park's centennial.

Cooke School

Cooke School has served as an integral part of the North Rosedale Park experience since it opened in 1926 with 217 students. A vote in October 1925 annexed Rosedale Park (then part of Redford Township) to the city of Detroit and put the new school under the control of the Detroit Board of Education. Unfortunately, the Detroit board inherited a school with a host of problems, including issues with heating, sewage and flooding. The other major problem: Cooke School was constructed by the Redford school board on land that it didn't own. In the end, the Detroit school board had to purchase the entire block for $21,900.

Mabelle Guilloz, a Detroit native and longtime employee of the school system, was the first principal, spending just a year there before transferring to the Dixon School. The school itself was named after Wayne County native Thomas Dale Cooke born in Flat Rock in October 1862. Additions to accommodate a gymnasium, auditorium and additional classrooms were constructed in 1937 and 1953.

Along with the Community House, Cooke anchored the neighborhood for the many families that lived there. However, court-ordered busing left it with only kindergarten through fifth grades, as sixth through eighth grades were sent to Cerveny in 1976. Many students shifted to parochial or private schools as a result. School choice further eroded Cooke's history as a neighborhood school.

In August 2006, about 200 former students held a reunion, attended by former principal Dr. Leonard Zudick, beloved teacher Dorothy Lynch, Spanish teacher Dorothy Koruga and physical education teacher Helen Cuscutis. In 2016, the name was changed to Cooke STEM Academy in recognition of its evolution to a science, technology, engineering, and mathematics focus. TCF Bank's decision in 2020 to fund a STEM lab at the school, as part of its overall commitment to the Grandmont Rosedale neighborhoods, bodes well for Cooke's future. – Daniel Bellware

The Legacy Project

The year was 2011. The Community House was approaching its 75th birthday and feeling its age. Its roof leaked. The patio was crumbling. Ruts marred the parking lot. There were no handicap-accessible restrooms. The lobby was too small for major events. It was time to address aging infrastructure and maintenance costs. Hence, the birth of The Legacy Project.

What evolved was an ambitious project developed from focus groups to a feasibility study and ultimately a $2.5-million campaign plan. Over 200 current and former residents and friends of North Rosedale Park participated on committees formed to implement a successful capital campaign – advisory, honorary, blue ribbon, fundraising, marketing, financial/legal, outreach, and architectural review – guided initially by a leadership committee and, in 2013, by a steering committee.

The NRPCA board approved a phased approach, beginning with construction of an addition on the south side of the Community House in 2015. Its welcoming lobby with glass windows facing the park and handicap-accessible restrooms now accommodates larger events and acts as additional meeting space. As a result, rentals have increased, helping to ensure its continuance as the historical heart of the community. Except for a one-year consultant funded by the Kresge Foundation, all fundraising was volunteer-driven.

Subsequent improvements included a new roof with solar panels and rebuilt circular drive and parking lot. A 2500-square-foot plaza added in 2018 adjacent to the lobby, featuring a major sculpture by Charles McGee and commemorative brick pavers, is now a favorite place for outdoor concerts and social events. The baseball diamond was regraded, equipment purchased for the soccer program, and improvements made to the playground. The last major upgrade was a new commercial kitchen in 2019. Installation of sidewalks, walking paths, and plaza rain gardens are pending.

Success followed success. Since 2013, the NRPCA has received five grants from the City of Detroit; seven from the State of Michigan, including five from the Michigan Council for Arts and Cultural Affairs; one each from the Knight Foundation, William Davidson Foundation and LISC; two from the Kresge Foundation; and over 400 contributions from individuals, corporations and businesses. In all, the campaign has raised more than $1.9 million for the improvements, close to $500,000 from individuals alone, a tremendous tribute to the commitment of the many involved and to the legacy of North Rosedale Park.

BIBLIOGRAPHY

1920s

1. Michigan State University Archaeology Program. "Following Grand River Avenue Through History." June 12, 2014. http://campusarch.msu.edu/?p=3076

2. Detroitmi.gov. 2020. Proposed Rosedale Park Historic District, Final Report. February 2007 https://detroitmi.gov/sites/detroitmi.localhost/files/2018-08/Rosedale%20Park%20HD%20Final%20 Report.pdf.

3. Detroitmi.gov. 2020. Proposed Rosedale Park Historic District, Final Report.

4. Caloia, Stefanie. "Annexation: A Promise of Paved Streets and Inside Toilets, Part II." Redford Township Historical Commission. June 22, 2016. https://redfordhistorical.com/2016/06/22/annexation-a-promise-of-paved-streets-and-inside-toilets-part-ii/

1930s

1. "Michigan History, How the Great Depression Changed Detroit." *The Detroit News*, March 3, 1999. http://blogs.detroitnews.com/history/1999/03/03/how-the-great-depression-changed-detroit/

2. Gillette, Gary. "A Sleeping Giant: Detroit in the Mid-1930s." Detroit the Unconquerable: The 1935 World Champion Tigers, Edited by Scott Ferkovich. Society for American Baseball Research: 2015

1940s

1. Eschner, Kat. "How Detroit Went from Motor City to the Arsenal of Democracy." *Smithsonian Magazine*, March 28, 2017. https://www.smithsonianmag.com/smart-news/when-detroit-was-arsenal-democracy-180962620/

2. Detroit Historical Society. Encyclopedia of Detroit: Arsenal of Democracy. https://detroithistorical.org/learn/encyclopedia-of-detroit/arsenal-democracy

3. Odlum, Floyd. "The Plight of Small Business." Credit Digest, November 27, 1941. Cited in *Rosedale Tattler*, December 1941.

4. NAACP Legal Defense Fund. "History of Housing Discrimination Against African Americans in Detroit." https://www.naacpldf.org/files/our-work/Detroit%20Housing%20Discrimination.pdf

5. Detroit Historical Society. Encyclopedia of Detroit: Race Riots of 1943. https://detroithistorical.org/learn/encyclopedia-of-detroit/race-riot-1943

6. Patterson, James T. Grand Expectations: The United States, 1945-1974. New York: Oxford University Press, 1996.

1950s

1. Padnani, Amy. "Anatomy of Detroit's Decline." *New York Times*, December 8, 2013. https://archive.nytimes.com/www.nytimes.com/interactive/2013/08/17/us/detroit-decline.html

2. Mc Graw, Bill. "Detroit 67: The Deep Scars the City Still Feels Today." *Detroit Free Press*, July 29, 2017. https://www.freep.com/story/news/detroitriot/2017/07/30/detroit-67-riot-race/512977001/

3. Austin, Dan. "Meet the 5 Worst Mayors in Detroit History." *Detroit Free Press*, Aug. 29, 2014. https://www.freep.com/story/news/local/2014/08/29/5-worst-mayors-in-detroit-history/14799541/

4. Austin, "Meet the 5 Worst Mayors in Detroit History."

5. Molner, Joseph G. and George H. Agate. "Final Report of Poliomyelitis Epidemic in Detroit and Wayne County, 1958." Public Health Reports (1896-1970) Vol. 75, No. 11 (November 1960). https://www.jstor.org/stable/4590995

1960s

1. Sugrue, Thomas J. The Origins of the Urban Crisis: Race and Inequality in Postwar Detroit. Princeton University Press, 2014.

2. Detroit Historical Society. Pattinson, William. "Detroit 1967 Oral and Written History Project." July 19, 2017. https://detroit1967.detroithistorical.org/items/show/594

3. Boissoneault, Lorraine. "Understanding Detroit's 1967 Upheaval 50 Years Later." *Smithsonian Magazine*, July 26, 2017. https://www.smithsonianmag.com/history/understanding-detroits-1967-upheaval-50-years-later-180964212/

1970s

1. Zhang, Mobei. WASPS. Wiley Online Library. December 30, 2015 https://doi.org/10.1002/9781118663202.wberen692

2. McGraw, Bill. "Coleman Young: The 10 Greatest Myths." *Detroit Free Press*, May 26, 2018. https://www.freep.com/story/opinion/2018/05/26/coleman-young-myths/638105002/

1980s

1. Chafets, Z'ev. "The Tragedy of Detroit." *New York Times Magazine*, July 29, 1990, page 23.

2. General Motors. "Detroit-Hamtramck to be GM's First Assembly Plant 100 Percent Devoted to Electric Vehicles." January 27, 2020. https://media.gm.com/media/us/en/gm/home.detail.html/content/Pages/news/us/en/2020/jan/0127-dham.html

3. Detroit Historical Society. Encyclopedia of Detroit: Fox Theatre https://detroithistorical.org/learn/encyclopedia-of-detroit/fox-theatre

Other sources include:

Rosedale Tattler, December 1926-December 2019.

St. John, Harry. "The Beginning of North Rosedale Park." *Rosedale Tattler*, October 1934-March 1937.

Hudson, Bill and Jack Lillie. A Quarter Century in North Rosedale Park. North Rosedale Park Civic Association, 1948.

ACKNOWLEDGMENTS

Although I have the privilege of being listed as the author, the development of this book was a team effort. Thank you to the current and former Park residents who shared their experiences, photos, and mementos. Your contributions were invaluable.

History Book Committee

I would like to acknowledge members of the history book committee, who started on this journey with me in early 2020. Their work made the writing so much easier. They include: (l-r) Wendy Jackson (NRPCA president), Marcia Closson (proofreader), Raymond Gregory (*Tattler* researcher), Nestelynn Garrett (book sales), Theresa Glenn (history researcher), Tess Tchou (book promotion), Melissa Poirier (photography), Amy Castillo (noted residents list), Eric Roth (*Tattler* researcher), Rose Love (author) and Marsha Bruhn (editor).

Not pictured: Deena Policicchio (consent form)

A thousand thank yous to Marsha Bruhn, who worked tirelessly with me in developing the book, editing copy, making suggestions and providing a ton of photos and documents for consideration.

Content Contributors – Daniel Bellware, Marsha Bruhn and Nestelynn Garrett

Photography and Document Contributors

David Edwards (cover photo of house and photos on page 5)

Melissa Poirier (photo organizer and photos of book and centennial committees)

James Martin (cover aerial photo)

Bernard Ball, Daniel Bellware, Marsha Bruhn, Chris Davis, Larry Davis, Susan Miller Erickson, Sally Evalt, Grandmont Rosedale Development Corporation, Sharon Lemieux, James Martin, Karen Moore, Tom Ridgway, Ray Tchou, Tess Tchou and Loyce Turpin

Centennial Committee

The Centennial Committee began planning for several events to recognize North Rosedale Park's 100th birthday in 2020, but plans were interrupted by the coronavirus. The committee includes: (l-r) Wendy Jackson (NRPCA president), Nestelynn Garrett (program), Marcia Closson (program), James Courtney (marketing), Theresa Glenn (research), Tess Tchou (co-chair), Gloria Goodwine (program), Carol Allen (budget), Marsha Bruhn (co-chair), and Rose Love (author).

Not pictured: Beverly Frederick (program), Bill Frey (legal), Adriane Henry (program), Julianne Lyons (historical marker), Joanna Ross (program) and David Utley (program)

Also, I would like to acknowledge my family and especially my husband, Darryl, and daughter and son-in-love, Rachel and Brandon Cottrell, for their encouragement and support. Last, I give honor to my Savior Jesus Christ for guidance, motivation and perseverance to complete the book.

About the Author

Rose M. Love is a communications professional with the City of Detroit, freelance writer and a former newspaper reporter with the Port Huron Times Herald. She has lived in North Rosedale Park since 1991 and has served as a block captain for several years and on the NRPCA Legacy Project steering committee since 2012. She is a graduate of Wayne State University and a member of Elim Baptist Church in Detroit. After learning that North Rosedale Park was 100 years old, she was so excited and quickly recommended a centennial celebration and development of a book to share the story of our wonderful neighborhood.

CPSIA information can be obtained
at www.ICGtesting.com
Printed in the USA
BVHW091638280221
601272BV00003B/8